HISTORY

OF THE

OTTAWA AND CHIPPEWA INDIANS

OF MICHIGAN

HISTORY

OF THE

OTTAWA AND

CHIPPEWA INDIANS

OF MICHIGAN;

A GRAMMAR OF THEIR LANGUAGE ,

AND PERSONAL AND FAMILY HISTORY OF THE AUTHOR

BY

ANDREW J. BLACKBIRD

KALPAZ

ISBN: 978-93-5128-605-9

First Published in 1887
Indian Reprint in 2017

Published by

Kalpaz Publications
C-30, Satyawati Nagar,elhi – 110052
E-mail: kalpaz@hotmail.com
Website: kalpazpublications.com
Ph.: +91-9212142040

Cataloging in Publication Data—DK
Courtesy: D.K. Agencies (P) Ltd. <docinfo@dkagencies.com>

Blackbird, Andrew J., 1810- **author.**
History of the Ottawa and Chippewa Indians of Michigan : a grammar of their language, and personal and family history of the author / by Andrew J. Blackbird.
pages cm
"First published in 1887"—Title page verso.
ISBN 9789351286059

1. Ottawa Indians—Michigan. 2. Ojibwa Indians—Michigan. 3. Ottawa language—Grammar. 4. Ojibwa language—Grammar. 5. Blackbird, Andrew J., 1810- I. Title.

E99.O9B53 2017 DDC 977.40049733 23

INTRODUCTION.

ANDREW J. BLACKBIRD, the author of this little book, is an educated Indian, son of the Ottawa Chief. His Indian name is Mack-aw-de-be-nessy (Black Hawk), but he generally goes by the name of "Blackbird," taken from the interpretation of the French "L'Oiseau noir." Mr. Blackbird's wife is an educated and intelligent white woman of English descent, and they have four children. He is a friend of the white people, as well as of his own people. Brought up as an Indian, with no opportunity for learning during his boyhood, when he came to think for himself, he started out blindly for an education, without any means but his brains and his hands.

He was loyal to the Government during the rebellion in the United States, for which cause he met much opposition by designing white people, who had full sway among the Indians, and who tried to mislead them and cause them to be disloyal; and he broke up one or two rebellious councils amongst his people during the progress of the rebellion.

When Hon. D. C. Leach, of Traverse City, Mich., was Indian Agent, Mr. Blackbird was appointed United States Interpreter and continued in this office with other subsequent Agents of the Department for many years. Before he was fairly out of this office, he was appointed postmaster of Little Traverse, now Harbor Springs, Mich., and faithfully discharged his duties as such for over eleven years with but very little salary.

He has also for several years looked after the soldiers' claims for widows and orphans, both for the whites as well as for his own people, in many instances without the least compensation, not even his stamps and paper paid. He is now decrepit with old age and failing health, and unable to perform hard manual labor.

We therefore recommend this work of Mr. A. J. Blackbird as interesting and reliable.

JAMES L. MORRICE,
Treasurer of Emmet County.

C. F. NEWKIRK,
Principal Harbor Springs Public Schools.

CHARLES R. WRIGHT,
Ex-President Harbor Springs.

CHARLES W. INGALLS,
Notary Public for Emmet Co.

ALBERT L. HATHAWAY,
County Clerk, Emmet County.

WM. H. LEE,
Probate Clerk and Abstractor of Titles.

ARCH. D. METZ,
Deputy Register of Deeds.

WILLARD P. GIBSON,
Pastor Presbyterian Church.

WILLIAM H. MILLER, U. S. A.

PREFACE.

I deem it not improper to present the history of the last race of Indians now existing in the State of Michigan, called the Ottawa and Chippewa Nations of Indians.

There were many other tribes of Indians in this region prior to the occupancy of the Ottawa and Chippewa Indians of this State, who have long ago gone out of existence. Not a page of their history is on record; but only an allusion to them in our traditions.

I have herewith recorded the earliest history of the Ottawa tribe of Indians in particular, according to their traditions. I have related where they formerly lived, the names of their leaders, and what tribes they contended with before and after they came to Michigan, and how they came to be the inhabitants of this State. Also the earliest history of the Island of Mackinac, and why it is called "Michilimackinac"— which name has never been correctly translated by white historians, but which is here given according to our knowledge of this matter long before we came in contact with white races.

I have also recorded some of the most important legends, which resemble the Bible history; particularly the legends with regard to the great flood, which has been in our language for many centuries, and the legend of the great fish which swallowed the prophet Ne-naw-bo-zhoo, who came out again alive, which might be considered as corresponding to the story of Jonah in the Sacred History.

Beside my own personal and our family history, I have also, quite extensively, translated our language into English and added many other items which might be interesting to all who may wish to inquire into our history and language.

ANDREW J. BLACKBIRD.

ACKNOWLEDGMENT.

The Ypsilanti Auxiliary of the Women's National Indian Association, by whose efforts this book is published, take this opportunity to express earnest thanks to those who have aided in this work.

Most generous donations of money from friends of Indians and equally valuable liberality from publishers and papermakers have made possible the preservation of this most rare and important history.

This is the only instance where a native Indian has recorded the story of his people and given a grammar of their language; thus producing a work whose immense value, as an account of a race and a language already passing into oblivion, will become even more inestimable with the lapse of time.

Ypsilanti, Mich., Oct., 1887.

CHAPTER I.

History of the Ottawas of Michigan—Preliminary Remarks in Regard to Other Histories, Concerning the Massacre of the Old British Fort on the Straits of Mackinac—British Promise to the Ottawas—Ravages of Small Pox—First Recollection of the Country of Arbor-Croche and Its Definition—Uprightness and Former Character of the Indians.

I have seen a number of writings by different men who attempted to give an account of the Indians who formerly occupied the Straits of Mackinac and Mackinac Island, (that historic little island which stands at the entrance of the strait,) also giving an account of the Indians who lived and are yet living in Michigan, scattered through the counties of Emmet, Cheboygan, Charlevoix, Antrim, Grand Traverse, and in the region of Thunder Bay, on the west shore of Lake Huron. But I see no very correct account of the Ottawa and Chippewa tribes of Indians, according to our knowledge of ourselves, past and present. Many points are far from being credible. They are either misstated by persons who were not versed in the traditions of these Indians, or exaggerated. An instance of this is found in the history of the life of Pontiac (pronounced Bwon-diac), the Odjebwe (or Chippewa) chief of St. Clair, the instigator of the massacre of the old fort on the Straits of Mackinac, written by a noted historian. In his account of the massacre, he says there was at this time no known surviving Ottawa Chief living on the south side of the Straits. This point of the history is incorrect, as there were several Ottawa chiefs living on the south side of the Straits at this particular time, who took no part in this massacre, but took by force the few survivors of this great, disastrous catastrophe, and protected them for a while and afterwards took them to Montreal, presenting them to the British Government; at the same time praying that their brother Odjebwes should not be retaliated upon on account of their rash act against the British people, but that they might be pardoned, as this terrible tragedy was committed through mistake, and through the evil counsel of one of their leaders by the name of Bwondiac (known in history as Pontiac). They told the British Government that their brother Odjebwes were few in number, while the British were in great numbers and daily increasing from an unknown part of the world across the ocean. They said, "Oh, my father, you are like the trees of the forest, and if one of the forest trees should be wounded with a hatchet, in a few years its wound will be entirely healed. Now, my father, compare with this: this is what my brother Odjebwe did to some of your children on the Straits of Mackinac, whose survivors we now bring back and present to your arms. O my father, have mercy upon my brothers and pardon them; for with your long arms and many, but a few strokes of retaliation would cause our brother to be entirely annihilated from the face of the earth!"

According to our understanding in our traditions, that was the time the British Government made such extraordinary promises to the Ottawa tribe of Indians, at the same time thanking them for their humane action upon those British remnants of the massacre. She promised them that her long arms will perpetually extend around them from generation to generation, or so long as there should be rolling sun. They should receive gifts from her sovereign in shape of goods, provisions, firearms, ammunition, and intoxicating liquors! Her sovereign's beneficent arm should be even extended unto the dogs belonging to the Ottawa tribe of Indians. And what place soever she should meet them, she would freely unfasten the faucet which contains her living water—whisky, which she will also cause to run perpetually and freely unto the Ottawas as the fountain of perpetual spring! And furthermore: she said, "I am as many as the stars in the heavens; and when you get up in the morning, look to the east; you will see that the sun, as it will peep through the earth, will be as red as my coat, to remind you why I am likened unto the sun, and my promises will be as perpetual as the rolling sun!"

Ego-me-nay—Corn-hanger—was the head counselor and speaker of the Ottawa tribe of Indians at that time, and, according to our knowledge, Ego-me-nay was the leading one who went with those survivors of the massacre, and he was the man who made the speech before the august assembly in the British council hall at Montreal at that time. Ne-saw-key—Down-the-hill—the head chief of the Ottawa Nation, did not go with the party, but sent his message, and instructed their counselor in what manner he should appear before the British Government. My father was a little boy at that time, and my grandfather and my great-grandfather were both living then, and both held the first royal rank among the Ottawas. My grandfather was then a sub-chief and my great-grandfather was a war chief, whose name was Pun-go-wish. And several other chiefs of the tribe I could mention who existed at that time, but this is ample evidence that the historian was mistaken in asserting that there was no known Ottawa chief existing at the time of the massacre.

However it was a notable fact that by this time the Ottawas were greatly reduced in numbers from what they were in former times, on account of the small-pox which they brought from Montreal during the French war with Great Britain. This small pox was sold to them shut up in a tin box, with the strict injunction not to open the box on their way homeward, but only when they should reach their country; and that this box contained something that would do them great good, and their people! The foolish people believed really there was something in the box supernatural, that would do them great good. Accordingly, after they reached home they opened the box; but behold there was another tin box inside, smaller. They took it out and opened the second box, and behold, still there was another box inside of the second box, smaller yet. So they kept on this way till they came to a very small box, which was not more than an inch long; and when they opened the last one they found nothing but mouldy particles in this last little box! They wondered very much what it was, and a great many closely inspected to try to find out what it meant. But alas, alas! pretty soon burst out a terrible sickness among them. The great Indian doctors themselves were taken sick and died. The tradition says it was indeed awful and terrible. Every one taken with it was sure to die. Lodge after lodge was totally vacated—nothing but the dead bodies lying here and there in their lodges—entire families being swept off with the ravages of this terrible disease. The whole coast of Arbor Croche, or Waw-gaw-naw-ke-zee, where their principal village was situated, on the west shore of the peninsula near the Straits, which is said to have been a continuous village some fifteen or sixteen miles long and extending from what is now called Cross Village to Seven-Mile Point (that is, seven miles from Little Traverse, now Harbor Springs), was entirely depopulated and laid waste. It is generally believed among the Indians of Arbor Croche that this wholesale murder of the Ottawas by this terrible disease sent by the British people, was actuated through hatred, and expressly to kill off the Ottawas and Chippewas because they were friends of the French Government or French King, whom they called "Their Great Father." The reason that to-day we see no full-grown trees standing along the coast of Arbor Croche, a mile or more in width along the shore, is because the trees were entirely cleared away for this famous long village, which existed before the small-pox raged among the Ottawas.

In my first recollection of the country of Arbor Croche,* which

* The word Arbor Croche is derived from two French words: Arbre, a tree; and Croche, something very crooked or hook-like. The tradition says when the Ottawas first came to that part of the country a great pine tree stood very near the shore where Middle Village now is, whose top was very crooked, almost hook-like. Therefore the Ottawas called the place "Wau-gaw-naw-ke-zee"—meaning the crooked top of the tree. But by and by the whole coast from Little Traverse to Tehin-gaw-beng, now Cross Village, became denominated as Wau-gaw-naw-ke-zee.

is sixty years ago, there was nothing but small shrubbery here and there in small patches, such as wild cherry trees, but the most of it was grassy plain; and such an abundance of wild strawberries, raspberries and blackberries that they fairly perfumed the air of the whole coast with fragrant scent of ripe fruit. The wild pigeons and every variety of feathered songsters filled all the groves, warbling their songs joyfully and feasting upon these wild fruits of nature; and in these waters the fishes were so plentiful that as you lift up the anchor-stone of your net in the morning, your net would be so loaded with delicious whitefish as to fairly float with all its weight of the sinkers. As you look towards the course of your net, you see the fins of the fishes sticking out of the water in every way. Then I never knew my people to want for anything to eat or to wear, as we always had plenty of wild meat and plenty of fish, corn, vegetables, and wild fruits. I thought (and yet I may be mistaken) that my people were very happy in those days, at least I was as happy myself as a lark, or as the brown thrush that sat daily on the uppermost branches of the stubby growth of a basswood tree which stood near by upon the hill where we often played under its shade, lodging our little arrows among the thick branches of the tree and then shooting them down again for sport.

Early in the morning as the sun peeped from the east, as I would yet be lying close to my mother's bosom, this brown thrush would begin his warbling songs perched upon the uppermost branches of the basswood tree that stood close to our lodge. I would then say to myself, as I listened to him, "here comes again my little orator," and I used to try to understand what he had to say; and sometimes thought I understood some of its utterances as follows: "Good morning, good morning! arise, arise! shoot, shoot! come along, come along!" etc., every word repeated twice. Even then, and so young as I was, I used to think that little bird had a language which God or the Great Spirit had given him, and every bird of the forest understood what he had to say, and that he was appointed to preach to other birds, to tell them to be happy, to be thankful for the blessings they enjoy among the summer green branches of the forest, and the plenty of wild fruits to eat. The larger boys used to amuse themselves by playing a ball called Paw-kaw-do-way, foot-racing, wrestling, bow-arrow shooting, and trying to beat one another shooting the greatest number of chipmunks and squirrels in a day, etc.

I never heard any boy or any grown person utter any bad language, even if they were out of patience with anything. Swearing or profanity was never heard among the Ottawa and Chippewa tribes of Indians, and not even found in their language. Scarcely any drunkenness, only once in a great while the old folks used to have a kind of short spree, particularly when there was any special occasion of a great feast going on. But all the young folks did not drink intoxicating liquors as a beverage in those days. And we always rested in perfect safety at night in our dwellings, and the doorways of our lodges had no fastenings to them, but simply a frail mat or a blanket was hung over our doorways which might be easily pushed or thrown one side without any noise if theft or any other mischief was intended. But we were not afraid for any such thing to happen us, because we knew that every child of the forest was observing and living under the precepts which their forefathers taught them, and the children were taught almost daily by their parents from infancy unto manhood and womanhood, or until they were separated from their families.

These precepts or moral commandments by which the Ottawa and Chippewa nations of Indians were governed in their primitive state, were almost the same as the ten commandments which the God Almighty himself delivered to Moses on Mount Sinai on tables of stone. Very few of these divine precepts are not found among the precepts of the Ottawa and Chippewa Indians, except with regard to the Sabbath day to keep it holy; almost every other commandment can be found, only there are more, as there were about twenty of these "uncivilized" precepts. They also believed, in their primitive state, that the eye of this Great Being is the sun by day, and by night the moon and stars, and, therefore, that God or the Great Spirit sees all things everywhere, night and day, and it would be impossible to hide our actions, either good or bad, from the eye of this Great Being. Even the very threshold or crevice of your wigwam will be a witness against you, if you should commit any criminal action when no human eye could observe your criminal doings, but surely your criminal actions will be revealed in some future time to your disgrace and shame. These were continual inculcations to the children by their parents, and in every feast and council, by the "Instructors of the Precepts" to the people or to the audience of the council. For these reasons the Ottawas and Chippewas in their primitive state were strictly honest and upright in their dealings with their fellow-beings. Their word of promise was as good as a promissory note, even better, as these notes sometimes are neglected and not performed according to their promises; but the Indian promise was very sure and punctual, although, as they had no timepieces, they measured their time by the sun. If an Indian promised to execute a certain obligation at such time, at so many days, and at such height of the sun, when that time comes he would be there punctually to fulfill this obligation. This was formerly the character of the Ottawa and Chippewa Indians of Michigan. But now, our living is altogether different, as we are continually suffering under great anxiety and perplexity, and continually being robbed and cheated in various ways. Our houses have been forcibly entered for thieving purposes and murder; people have been knocked down and robbed; great safes have been blown open with powder in our little town and their contents carried away, and even children of the Caucasian race are heard cursing and blaspheming the name of their Great Creator, upon whose pleasure we depended for our existence.

According to my recollection of the mode of living in our

village, so soon as darkness came in the evening, the young boys and girls were not allowed to be out of their lodges. Every one of them must be called in to his own lodge for the rest of the night. And this rule of the Indians in their wild state was implicitly observed.

Ottawa and Chippewa Indians were not what we would call entirely infidels and idolaters; for they believed that there is a Supreme Ruler of the Universe, the Creator of all things, the Great Spirit, to which they offer worship and sacrifices in a certain form. It was customary among them, every spring of the year, to gather all the cast off garments that had been worn during the winter and rear them up on a long pole while they were having festivals and jubilees to the Great Spirit. The object of doing this was that the Great Spirit might look down from heaven and have compassion on his red children. Only this, that they foolishly believe that there are certain deities all over the lands who to a certain extent govern or preside over certain places, as a deity who presides over this river, over this lake, or this mountain, or island, or country, and they were careful not to express anything which might displease such deities; but that they were not supreme rulers, only to a certain extent they had power over the land where they presided. These deities were supposed to be governed by the Great Spirit above.

CHAPTER II.

Cases of Murders Among the Ottawas and Chippewas Exceedingly Scarce—Ceding the Grand Traverse Region to the Chippewas on Account of Murder—Immorality Among the Ottawas not Common—Marriage in Former Times.

The murders in cold blood among the Ottawa and Chippewa nations of Indians in their primitive state were exceedingly few, at least there was only one account in our old tradition where a murder had been committed, a young Ottawa having stabbed a young Chippewa while in dispute over their nets when they were fishing for herrings on the Straits of Mackinac. This nearly caused a terrible bloody war between the two powerful tribes of Indians (as they were numerous then) so closely related. The tradition says they had council after council upon this subject, and many speeches were delivered on both sides. The Chippewas proposed war to settle the question of murder, while the Ottawas proposed compromise and restitution for the murder. Finally the Ottawas succeeded in settling the difficulty by ceding part of their country to the Chippewa nation, which is now known and distinguished as the Grand Traverse Region. A strip of land which I believe to have extended from a point near Sleeping Bear, down to the eastern shore of the Grand Traverse Bay, some thirty or forty miles wide, thence between two parallel lines running southeasterly until they strike the head waters of Muskegon River, which empties into Lake Michigan not very far below Grand Haven. They were also allowed access to all the rivers and streams in the Lower Peninsula of Michigan, to trap the beavers, minks, otters and muskrats. The Indians used their furs in former times for garments and blankets. This is the reason that to this day the Odjebwes (Chippewas) are found in that section of the country.

It may be said, this is not true; it is a mistake. We have known several cases of murders among the Ottawas and Chippewas. I admit it to be true, that there have been cases of murders among the Ottawas and Chippewas since the white people knew them. But these cases of murders occurred some time after they came in contact with the white races in their country; but I am speaking now of the primitive condition of Indians, particularly of the Ottawas and Chippewas, and I believe most of those cases of murders were brought on through the bad influence of white men, by introducing into the tribes this great destroyer of mankind, soul and body, intoxicating liquors! Yet, during sixty years of my existence among the Ottawas and Chippewas, I have never witnessed one case of murder of this kind, but I heard there were a few cases in other parts of the country, when in their fury from the influence of intoxicating liquors.

There was one case of sober murder happened about fifty years ago at Arbor Croche, where one young man disposed of his lover by killing, which no Indian ever knew the actual cause of. He was arrested and committed to the Council and tried according to the Indian style; and after a long council, or trial, it was determined the murderer should be banished from the tribe. Therefore, he was banished. Also, about this time, one case of sober murder transpired among the Chippewas of Sault Ste. Marie, committed by one of the young Chippewas whose name was Wau-bau-ne-me-kee (White-thunder), who might have been released if he had been properly tried and impartial judgment exercised over the case, but we believe it was not. This Indian killed a white man, when he was perfectly sober, by stabbing. He was arrested, of course, and tried and sentenced to be hung at the Island of Mackinac. I distinctly remember the time. This poor Indian was very happy when he was about to be hung on the gallows. He told the people that he was very happy to die, for he felt that he was innocent. He did not deny killing the man, but he thought he was justifiable in the sight of the

Great Spirit, as such wicked monsters ought to be killed from off the earth; as this white man came to the Indian's wigwam in the dead of night, and dragged the mother of his children from his very bosom for licentious purpose. He remonstrated, but his remonstrances were not heeded, as this ruffian was encouraged by others who stood around his wigwam, and ready to fall upon this poor Indian and help their fellow-ruffian; and he therefore stabbed the principal party, in defence of his beloved wife, for which cause the white man died. If an Indian should go to the white man's house and commit that crime, he would be killed; and what man is there who would say that is too bad, this Indian to be killed in that manner? But every man will say amen, only he ought to have been tortured before he was killed; and let the man who killed this bad and wicked Indian be rewarded! This is what would be the result if the Indian would have done the same thing as this white man did.

The Ottawas and Chippewas were quite virtuous in their primitive state, as there were no illegitimate children reported in our old traditions. But very lately this evil came to exist among the Ottawas—so lately that the second case among the Ottawas of Arbor Croche is yet living. And from that time this evil came to be quite frequent, for immorality has been introduced among these people by evil white persons who bring their vices into the tribes.

In the former times or before the Indians were christianized, when a young man came to be a fit age to get married, he did not trouble himself about what girl he should have for his wife; but the parents of the young man did this part of the business. When the parents thought best that their son should be separated from their family by marriage, it was their business to decide what woman their son should have as his wife; and after selecting some particular girl among their neigbors, they would make up quite large package of presents and then go to the parents of the girl and demand the daughter for their son's wife, at the same time delivering the presents to the parents of the girl. If the old folks say yes, then they would fetch the girl right along to their son and tell him, We have brought this girl as your wife so long as you live; now take her, cherish her, and be kind to her so long as you live. The young man and girl did not dare to say aught against it, as it was the law and custom amongst their people, but all they had to do was to take each other as man and wife. This was all the rules and ceremony of getting married in former times among the Ottawas and Chippewas of Michigan: they must not marry their cousins nor second cousins.

CHAPTER III.

Earliest Possible Known History of Mackinac Island—Its Historical Definition—Who Resided at the Island—Massacre at the Island by Senecas—Where the Ottawas were Living at That Time—Only Two Escape the Massacre—What Became of Them—The Legends of the Two Who Escaped—Occupants of the Island Afterwards—Who Killed Warrior Tecumseh?

Again, most every historian, or annalist so-called, who writes about the Island of Mackinac and the Straits and vicinity, tells us that the definition or the meaning of the word "Michilimackinac" in the Ottawa and Chippewa language, is "large turtle," derived from the word Mi-she-mi-ki-nock in the Chippewa language. That is, "Mi-she" as one of the adnominals or adjectives in the Ottawa and Chippewa languages, which would signify tremendous in size; and "Mikinock" is the name of mud turtle—meaning, therefore, "monstrous large turtle," as the historians would have it. But we consider this to be a clear error. Whereever those annalists, or those who write about the Island of Mackinac, obtain their information as to the definition of the word Michilimackinac, I don't know, when our tradition is so direct and so clear with regard to the historical definition of that word, and is far from being derived from the word "Michimikinock," as the historians have told us. Our tradition says that when the Island was first discovered by the Ottawas, which was some time before America was known as an existing country by the white man, there was a small independent tribe, a remnant race of Indians who occupied this island, who became confederated with the Ottawas when the Ottawas were living at Manitoulin, formerly called Ottawa Island, which is situated north of Lake Huron. The Ottawas thought a good deal of this unfortunate race of people, as they were kind of interesting sort of people; but, unfortunately, they had most powerful enemies, who every now and then would come among them to make war with them. Their enemies were of the Iroquois of New York. Therefore, once in the dead of the winter while the Ottawas were having a great jubilee and war dances at their island, now Manitoulin, on account of the great conquest over the We-ne-be-goes of Wisconsin, of which I will speak more fully in subsequent chapters, during which time the Senecas of New York, of the Iroquois family of Indians, came upon the remnant race and fought them, and almost entirely annihilated them. But two escaped to tell the story, who effected their escape by flight and by hiding in one of the natural caves at the island, and therefore that was the end of this race. And according to our understanding and traditions the tribal name of those disastrous people was "Mi-shi-ne-macki naw-go," which is still existing to this day as a monument of their former existence; for the Ottawas and Chippewas named this little island "Mi-shi-ne-macki-nong" for memorial sake of those their former confederates, which word is the locative case of the Indian noun "Michinemackinawgo." Therefore, we contend, this is properly where the name Michilimackinac is originated.

This is the earliest possible history of this little Island, as I have related, according to the Ottawa traditions; and from that time forward there have been many changes in its history, as other tribes of Indians took possession of the island, such as the Hurons and Chippewas; and still later by the whites—French, English, and Americans; and numbers of battles have been fought from time to time there, by both Indians and whites, of which I need not relate as other historians have already given us the accounts of them. But only this I would relate, because I have never yet seen the account of it: It is related in our traditions that at the time when the Chippewas occupied the island they ceded it to the United States Government, but reserved a strip of land all around the island as far as a stone throw from its water's edge as their encampment grounds when they might come to the island to trade or for other business.

Perhaps the reader would like to know what became of those two persons who escaped from the lamented tribe Mishinemackinawgoes. I will here give it just as it is related in our traditions, although this may be considered, at this age, as a fictitious story; but every Ottawa and Chippewa to this day believes it to be positively so. It is related that the two persons escaped were two young people, male and female, and they were lovers. After everything got quieted down, they fixed their snow-shoes inverted and crossed the lake on the ice, as snow was quite deep on the ice, and they went towards the north shore of Lake Huron. The object of inverting their snow-shoes was that in case any person should happen to come across their track on the ice, their track would appear as if going towards the island. They became so disgusted with human nature, it is related, that they shunned every mortal being, and just lived by themselves, selecting the wildest part of the country. Therefore, the Ottawas and Chippewas called them "Paw-gwa-tchaw-nish-naw-boy." The last time they were seen by the Ottawas, they had ten children—all boys, and all living and well. And every Ottawa and Chippewa believes to this day that they are still in existence and roaming in the wildest part of the land, but as supernatural beings—that is, they can be seen or unseen, just as they see fit to be; and sometimes they simply manifested themselves as being present by throwing a club or a stone at a person walking in a solitude, or by striking a dog belonging to the person walking; and sometimes by throwing a club at the lodge, night or day, or hearing their footsteps walking around the wigwam when the Indians would be camping out in an unsettled part of the country, and the dogs would bark, just as they would bark at any strange person approaching the door. And sometimes they would be tracked on snow by hunters, and if followed on their track, however recently passed, they never could be overtaken. Sometimes when an Indian would be hunting or walking in solitude, he would suddenly be seized with an unearthly fright, terribly awe stricken, apprehending some great evil. He feels very peculiar sensation from head to foot--the hair of his head standing and feeling stiff like a porcupine quill. He feels almost benumbed with fright, and yet he does not know what it is; and looking in every direction to see something, but nothing to be seen which might cause sensation of terror. Collecting himself, he would then say, "Pshaw! its nothing here to be afraid of. It's nobody else but Paw-gwa-tchaw-nish-naw-boy is approaching me. Perhaps he wanted something of me." They would then leave something on their tracks—tobacco, powder, or something else. Once in a great while they would appear, and approach the person to talk with him, and in this case, it is said, they would always begin with the sad story of their great catastrophe at the Island of Mackinac. And whoever would be so fortunate as to meet and see them and to talk with them, such person would always become a prophet to his people, either Ottawa or Chippewa. Therefore, Ottawas and Chippewas called these supernatural beings "Paw-gwa-tchaw-nish-naw-boy," which is, strictly, "Wild roaming supernatural being."

Pine river country, in Charlevoix County, Michigan, when this country was all wild, especially near Pine Lake, was once considered as the most famous resort of these kind of unnatural beings. I was once conversing with one of the first white settlers of that portion of the country, who settled near to the place now called Boyne City, at the extreme end of the east arm of Pine Lake. In the conversation he told me that many times they had been frightened, particularly during the nights, by hearing what sounded like human footsteps around outside of their cabin; and their dog would be terrified, crouching at the doorway, snarling and growling, and sometimes fearfully barking. When daylight came, the old man would go out in order to discover what it was or if he could track anything around his cabin, but he never could discover a track of any kind. These remarkable, mischievous, audible, fanciful, appalling apprehensions were of very frequent occurrence before any other inhabitants or settlers came near to his place; but now, they do not have such apprehensions since many settlers came.

That massacre of Mishinimackinawgoes by Seneca Indians of New York happened probably more than five or six hundred years ago. I could say much more which would be contradictory of other writers of the history of the Indians in this country. Even in the history of the United States I think there are some mistakes concerning the accounts of the Indians, particularly the accounts of our brave Tecumseh, as it is claimed that he was killed by a soldier named Johnson, upon whom they conferred the honor of having disposed of the dreaded Tecumseh. Even pictured out as being coming up with his tomahawk to strike a man who was on horseback, but being instantly shot dead with the pistol. Now I have repeatedly heard our oldest Indians, both male and female, who were present at the defeat of the British and Indians, all tell a unanimous story, saying that they came to a clearing or opening spot, and it was there where Tecumseh ordered his warriors to rally and fight the Americans once more, and in this very spot one of the American musket balls took effect in Tecumseh's leg so as to break the bone of his leg, that he could not stand up. He was sitting on the ground when he told his warriors to flee as well as they could, and furthermore said, "One of my leg is shot off! But leave me one or two guns loaded; I am going to have a last shot. Be quick and go!" That was the last word spoken by Tecumseh. As they look back, they saw the soldiers thick as swarm of bees around where Tecumseh was sitting on the ground with his broken leg, and so they did not see him any more; and, therefore, we always believe that the Indians or Americans know not who made the fatal shot on Tecumseh's leg, or what the soldiers did with him when they came up to him as he was sitting on the ground.

CHAPTER IV.

The Author's Reasons for Recording the History of His People, and Their Language—History of His Nationality—A Sketch of His Father's History—How the Indians Were Treated in Manitoba Country One Hundred Years Ago—His Father's Banishment to Die on a Lonely Island by the White Traders—Second Misfortune of the Ottawas on Account of the Shawanee Prophet—The Earthquake.

The Indian tribes are continnually diminishing on the face of this continent. Some have already passed entirely out of existence and are forgotten, who once inhabited this part of the country; such as the Mawsh-ko-desh, Urons, Ossaw-gees—who formerly occupied Saw-gi-naw-bay; and the Odaw gaw-mees, whose principal habitation was about the vicinity of Detroit River. They are entirely vanished into nothingness. Not a single page of their history can be found on record in the history of this country, or hardly an allusion to their existence. My own race, once a very numerous, powerful and warlike tribe of Indians, who proudly trod upon this soil, is also near the end of existence. In a few more generations they will be so intermingled with the Caucasian race as to be hardly distinguished as descended from the Indian nations, and their language will be lost. I myself was brought up in a pure Indian style, and lived in a wigwam, and have partaken of every kind of the wild jubilees of my people, and was once considered one of the best "Pipe" dancers of the tribe. But when nearly grown up, I was invited by a traveling Protestant Missionary, whose name was Alvin Coe, to go home with him to the State of Ohio, with the assurance that he would give me a good education like the white man, and the idea struck me that I could be really educated and be able to converse with the white people. And although at that time (in the fall of

1840) I missed the opportnnity, the idea was never after off of my mind. So some time afterwards I started out voluntarily to obtain an education; and I had nearly succeeded in completing my professional studies when I called away to come home and look after my aged father, in 1850. And now I have four children, but not one of them can speak the Indian language. And every one of the little Indian urchins who are now running about in our town can speak to each other quite fluently in the English language; but I am very sorry to add that they have also learned profanity like the white children. For these reasons it seems desirable that the history of my people should not be lost, like that of other tribes who previously existed in this country, and who have left no record of their ancient legends and their traditions.

Before proceeding to record the history of the Ottawas of the State of Michigan, to whom I am immediately connected in their common interests and their future destinies, I propose to rehearse in a summary manner my nationality and family history. Our tradition says that long ago, when the Ottawa tribes of Indians used to go on a warpath either towards the south or towards the west, even as far as to the Rocky Mountains, on one of these expeditions towards the Rocky Mountains my remote ancestors were captured and brought to this country as prisoners of war. But they were afterwards adopted as children of the Ottawas, and intermarried with the nation in which they were captives. Subsequently these captives' posterity became so famous among the Ottawas on account of their exploits and bravery on the warpath and being great hunters that they became closely connected with the royal families, and were considered as the best counselors, best chieftains and best warriors among the Ottawas. Thus I am not regularly descendad from the Ottawa nations of Indians, but I am descended, as tradition says, from the tribe in the far west known as the Underground race of people. They were so called on account of making their habitations in the ground by making holes large enough for dwelling pnrposes. It is related that they even made caves in the ground in which to keep their horses every night to prevent them from being stolen by other tribes who were their enemies. It is also related that they were quite an intelligent class of people. By cultivating the soil they raised corn and other vegetables to aid in sustaining life beside hunting and fishing. They were entirely independent, having their own government and language, and possessing their own national emblem which distinguished them as distinct and separate from all other tribes. This symbolical ensign of my ancestors was represented by a species of small hawk, which the Ottawas called the "Pe-pe-gwen." So we were sometimes called in this country in which we live the "Pe-pe-gwen tribe," instead of the "Undergrounds." And it was customary among the Ottawas, that if any one of our number, a descendant of the Undergrounds, should commit any punishable crime, all the Pe-pe-gwen tribe or descendants of the Undergrounds would be called together in a grand council and requested to make restitution for the crime or to punish the guilty one, according to the final decision of the council.

There were several great chieftains of the Undergrounds among the Ottawas who were living within my time, and some are here mentioned who were most known by the American people, particularly during the war with Great Britain in 1812. Most of these chieftains were my own uncles. One was called Late Wing, who took a very active part for the cause of the United States in the war of 1812, and he was a great friend to Governor Lewis Cass of Michigan. Wing was pensioned for life for his good services to the United States. He was one of my father's own brothers. Shaw-be-nee was an uncle of mine on my mother's side, who also served bravely for the United States in the war of 1812. He traveled free all over the United States during his lifetime. This privilege was granted to him by the Government of the United States for his patriotism and bravery. He died in the State of Illinois about twenty years ago from this writing, and a monument was raised for him by the people in that State. Wa-ke-zoo was another great chieftain who died before my time in the country of Manitoba, out north. He was also one of my father's brothers. It is related that he was also a prophet and a great magician.

My own dear father was one of the head chiefs at Arbor Croche, now called Middle Village or Good Heart, which latter name was given at my suggestion by the Postoffice Department at Washington. My father died in June, 1861. His Indian name was Macka-de-pe-nessy,* which means Black Hawk; but somehow it has been mistranslated into Blackbird, so we now go by this latter name. My father was a very brave man. He has led his warriors several times on the warpath, and he was noted as one who was most daring and adventurous in his younger days. He stayed about twenty years in the country of Manitoba with his brother Wa-ke-zoo, among other tribes of Indians and white fur-traders in that section of the country. Many times he has grappled with and narrowly escaped from the grizzly bear and treacherous buffalo which were then very numerous in that portion of the country. This was about one hundred years ago. He has seen there things that would be almost incredible at this present age: liquor sold to the Indians measured with a woman's thimble, a thimbleful for one dollar; one wooden coarse comb for two beaver skins; a double handful of salt for one beaver skin—and so on in proportion in everything else; the poor Indian had to give pile upon pile of beaver skins, which might be worth two or three hundred dollars, for a few yards of flimsy cloth. Englishmen and Frenchman who went there expressly to traffic with the Indians, generally started from Quebec and Montreal, leaving their families at home; but so soon as they reached this wild country, they would take Indian wives. When they left the country, they would leave their Indian wives and chil-

* This name is written variously, the letters d, b, t, and p, being considered identical in the Ottawa language.—[Ed.

dren there to shift for themselves. Consequently there are in this region thousands of half breeds, most beautiful men and beautiful women, but they are as savage as the rest of the Indians. No white man there ever told these poor Indians anything about Christianity, but only added unto them their degradations and robbed them.

My father was once there left to perish on a lonely island by the fur traders, not because he had done any crime, but simply from inhuman cruelty and disregard of Indians by these white men. He was traveling with these traders from place to place in a long bark canoe, which was the only means of conveyance on the water in those days. It appears that there were two parties, and two of these long bark canoes were going in the same direction, one of which my father was paddling for them. He was not hired, but simply had joined them in his travels. But these two parties were thrown into a great quarrel about who should have my father to paddle their canoe. Therefore they landed on this little island expressly to fight amongst themselves; and after fighting long and desperately, they left my poor father on this little island to die, for they concluded that neither of them should take him into their canoe. He was left to die! What must be the feelings of this poor Indian, to whom life was as sweet as to any human creature? What revenge should he take upon those traders? He had a gun, which he leveled at them as they started off in their canoes. His fingers were on the trigger, when suddenly a thought flashed across his mind—"Perhaps the Great Spirit will be displeased." So he dropped his gun, and raised a fervent prayer to the Almighty Ruler for deliverance from this awful situation. After being several days on this little island, when almost dying from starvation, fortunately deliverance came. He spied a small canoe with two persons in it within hail. They came and took him off from his dying situation. It was an Indian woman with her little son who happened to travel in that direction who saved my father's life.

From this time hence my father lost all confidence in white men, whatever the position or profession of the white man might be, whether a priest, preacher, lawyer, doctor, merchant, or common white man. He told us to beware of them, as they all were after one great object, namely, to grasp the world's wealth. And in order to obtain this, they would lie, steal, rob, or murder, if it need be; therefore he instructed us to beware how the white man would approach us with very smooth tongue, while his heart is full of deceit and far from intending to do us any good.

He left Manitoba country about 1800, or about the time when the Shawanee prophet, "Waw-wo-yaw-ge-she-maw," who was one of Tecumseh's own brothers, sent his emissaries to preach to the Ottawas and Chippewas in the Lower and Upper Peninsulas of Michigan, who advised the Ottawas and Chippewas to confess their sins and avow their wrongs and go west, and there to worship the Great Spirit according to the old style as their forefathers did,* and to abandon everything else which the white man had introduced into the tribes of Indians, to abandon even the mode of making fire, which was by flint and steel, and to start their fires by friction between the two pieces of dry wood as their forefathers made their fires before the white people came to this country, and to eat no flesh of domestic animals, but to eat nothing but wild game, and use their skins for their wearing apparel and robes as the Great Spirit designed them to be when He created them. He taught them that the Great Spirit was angry with them because they conformed to the habits of the white man, and that if they did not believe and practice the old habits, the Great Spirit would shake the earth as an evidence that he tells them the truth. A great many Ottawas believed and went far west accordingly. And it happened about this time the earth did

* The worship of the Great Spirit consisted mostly in songs and dancing accompanied with an Indian drum, which has a very deep and solemn sound, alnot very large, about a foot in diameter. I used to think that the sound of it must reach to the heaven where the Great Spirit is.

quake in Michigan; I think, if I am not mistaken, the earth shook twice within a year, which is recorded in the annals of this country. At the earthquake many Indians were frightened, and consequently many more believed and went west; but nearly all of them died out there because the climate did not agree with them. Saw-gaw-kee—Growing-plant—was the head chief of the Ottawa nation of Indians at that time, and was one of the believers who went with the parties out west, and he also died there.* This is the second time that the Ottawas were terribly reduced in numbers in the country of Arbor Croche.

---

*This Chief Saw-gaw-kee was Ne-saw-wa-quat's father, the last head chief of Little Traverse. Ne-saw-wa-quat was the only child remaining alive of the whole family of Saw-gaw-kee. Therefore the child was brought back to this country and was the last head chief of Little Traverse, now Harbor Springs.

CHAPTER V.

The Author's Father Appointed Speaker for the Ottawas and Chippewas—The Only Ottawa Who was Friendly to Education—Making Alphabet—Acting as School Teacher—Moving Disposition of the Ottawas—Mode of Traveling—Tradition of William Blackbird Being Fed by Angelic Beings in the Wilderness—His being Put into Mission School by His Father—Studying to be a Priest—His Assassination in the City of Rome, Italy, Almost the Day When He was to be Ordained—Memorial Poem—The Author's Remarks on the Death of His Brother.

After my father's return to Arbor Croche, he became quite an orator, and consequently he was appointed as the head speaker in the council of the Ottawa and Chippewa Indians. He continued to hold this office until his frame was beginning to totter with age, his memory became disconnected and inactive, and he therefore gave up his office to his own messenger, whose name was Joseph As-saw-gon, who died during the late rebellion in the United States while Hon. D. C. Leach, of Traverse City, was the Michigan Indian Agent. As-saw-gon was indeed quite an orator, considering his scanty opportunities. He had no education at all, but was naturally gifted as an orator. He was quite logical and allegorical in his manner of speaking. I have heard several white people remark, who had listened to his speeches through the imperfect interpreters, that he was as good a speaker as any orator who had been thoroughly educated.

My father was the only man who was friendly to education. When I was a little boy, I remember distinctly his making his own alphabet, which he called "Paw-pa-pe-po." With this he learned how to read and write; and afterwards he taught other Indians to read and write according to his alphabet. He taught no children, but only the grown persons. Our wigwam, which was about sixty or seventy feet long, where we lived in the summer time, was like a regular school-house, with my father as teacher of the school, and they had merry times in it. Many Indians came there to learn his Paw-pa-pe-po, and some of them were very easy to learn, while others found learning extremely difficult.

We were ten of us children in the family, six boys and four girls. I was the youngest of all who were living at that time. The eldest boy was one of the greatest hunters among the Ottawas. His name was Pung-o-wish, named after our great-grandfather, but he was afterwards called Peter by the Catholic missionaries when he was baptised into the Catholic religion. One of my brothers who was five or six years younger than my eldest brother was a remarkably interesting boy. His name was Petaw-wan-e-quot, though he was afterwards called William. He was quick to learn Paw-pa-pe-po, and very curious and interesting questions he would often ask of his father, which would greatly puzzle the old man to answer.

All the Indians of Arbor Croche used only to stay there during the summer time, to plant their corn, potatoes, and other vegetables. As soon as their crops were put away in the ground,* they would start all together towards the south, going to different points, some going as far as Chicago expressly to trap the muskrats, beavers, and many other kinds of furs, and others to the St. Joe River, Black River, Grand River, or Muskegon River, there to trap and hunt all winter, and make sugar in the spring. After sugar making they would come back again to Waw-gaw-naw-kezee, or Arbor Croche, to spend the summer and to raise their crops again as before.

* The mode of securing their corn was first to dry the ears by fire. When perfectly dry, they would then beat them with a flail and pick all the cobs out. The grain was then winnowed and put into sacks. These were put in the ground in a large cylinder made out of elm bark, set in deep in the ground and made very dry, filling this cylinder full and then covering it to stay there for winter and summer use.

In navigating Lake Michigan they used long bark canoes in which they carried their whole families and enough provisions to last them all winter. These canoes were made very light, out of white birch bark, and with a fair wind they could skip very lightly on the waters, going very fast, and could stand a very heavy sea. In one day they could sail quite a long distance along the coast of Lake Michigan. When night overtook them they would land and make wigwams with light poles of cedar which they always carried in their canoes. These wigwams were covered with mats made for that purpose out of prepared marsh reeds or flags sewed together, which made very good shelter from rain and wind, and were very warm after making fires inside of them. They had another kind of mat to spread on the ground to sit and sleep on. These mats are quite beautifully made out of different colors, and closely woven, of well prepared bull-rushes.* After breakfast in the morning they are off again in the big canoes.

My father's favorite winter quarters were somewhere above Big Rapids on Muskegon River. He hunted and trapped there all winter and made sugar. A very mysterious event happened to my brother William while my folks were making sugar there. One beautiful morning after the snow had entirely disappeared in the woods, my brother William, then at the age of about eight or nine years, was shooting around with his little bow and arrows among the sugar trees, but that day he never came home. At sundown, our parents were beginning to feel very uneasy about their little boy, and yet they thought he must have gone to some neighboring sugar bush, as there were quite a number of families also making sugar in the vicinity. Early in the morning, my father went to all the neighboring sugar camps, but William was nowhere to be found. So at once a search was instituted. Men

*To prepare these bull-rushes for mats, they are cut when very green, and then they go through the process of steaming, after bleaching by the sun; they are colored before they are woven. They are generally made about six or eight feet long and about four feet wide.

and boys were out in search for the boy, calling and shooting their guns far and near, but not a trace of him anywhere could be found. Our parents were almost distracted with anxiety and fear about their boy, and they continued the search three days in vain. On the fourth day, one of our cousins, whose name was Oge-maw-we-ne-ne, came to a very deep gully between two hills. He went up to the top of the highest hill in order to be heard a long distance. When he reached the top, he began to halloo as loud as he could, calling the child by name, Pe-taw-on-e-quot. At the end of his shouting he thought he heard some one responding to his call, "Wau?" This word is one of the interrogatives in the Indian language, and is equivalent to "what" in the English language. He listened a few minutes, and again he called as before, and again heard distinctly the same response, "Wau?" It came from above, right over his head, and as he looked upwards he saw the boy, almost at the top of a tree, standing on a small limb in a very dangerous situation. He said, "Hello, what are you doing up there? Can't you come down?" "Yes, I can," was the answer; "I came up here to find out where I am, and which way is our sugar camp." "Come down, then; I will show you which way is your home." After he came down from the tree, our cousin offered him food, but the child would not touch a morsel, saying that he was not hungry as he had eaten only a little while ago. "Ah, you have been fed then. Who fed you? We have been looking for you now over three days." The boy replied, "I had every thing that I wanted to eat in the great festival of the "Wa-me-te-go-zhe-wog." which is "the white people." "Where are they now?" asked our cousin. "That is just what I would like to know, too," said the boy; "I had just come out of their nice house between the two hills, and as I looked back after I came out of their door I saw no more of their house, and heard no more of them nor their music." Our cousin again questioned the boy, "How did you come to find these Wa-me-te-go-zhe-wog here?" And little William replied, "Those Wa-me-te-go-zhe-wog came to our sugar camp and invited me to go with them, but I thought it was very close by. I thought we walked only just a few steps to come to their door." Our cousin believed it was some supernatural event and hastened to take the boy to his anxious parents. Again and again little William told the same story when interrogated by any person, and it is firmly believed by all our family and friends that he was cherished and fed three days in succession by angelic beings.

When he was about twelve or thirteen years of age the Protestant Mission School started at Mackinac Island, and my father thought best to put him to that school. After being there less than a year, he was going around with his teachers, acting as interpreter among the Indian camps at the Island of Mackinac. I was perfectly astonished to see how quick he had acquired the English language. After the mission broke up at the island, about the time the Catholic mission was established at Little Traverse, William came home and stayed with us for about two years, when he was again taken by Bishop Reese with his little sister, a very lovely girl, whom the white people call Auntie Margaret, or Queen of the Ottawas. They were taken down to Cincinnati, Ohio, where they were put into higher schools, and there my brother attained the highest degree of education, or graduation as it is called.

From thence he was taken across the ocean to the city of Rome, Italy, to study for the priesthood, leaving his little sister in Cincinnati. It is related that he was a very eloquent and powerful orator, and was considered a very promising man by the people of the city of Rome, and received great attention from the noble families, on account of his wisdom and talent and his being a native American; and yet he had a much lighter complexion than his cousin Aug Hamlin, who was also taken over there and represented as half French.

While he was at Rome, the proposition arose in this country to buy out the Michigan Indians by the Government of the United

States, and he wrote to his people at Arbor Croche and to Little Traverse on this very subject, advising them not to sell out nor make any contract with the United States Government, but to hold on until he could return to America, when he would endeavor to aid them in making out the contract or treaty with the United States. Never to give up, not even if they should be threatened with annihilation or to be driven away at the point of the bayonet from their native soil. I wish I could produce some of this correspondence, but only one letter from him can now be found, which is here given:

ROME, April 17, 1833

MY DEAR SISTER:

It is a long time since I wrote you a few lines. I would write oftener if the time would permit, but I have very few leisure moments. However, as we have a holiday to-day, I determine to write a line or two. I have to attend to my studies from morning till sunset. I thank you very much for your kind letter which I received some time ago by politeness of Rev. Mr. Seajean. My dearest sister, you may have felt lost after I left you; you must consider who loves you with all the affection of parents. What can we return to those who have done us much good, but humble prayers for them that the Almighty may reward them for the benefit they have done in this poor mortal world. I was very happy when informed by Father Mullen that you had received six premiums at the examination; nothing else would more impress my heart than to hear of the success of your scholastic studies. I entreat you, dearest sister, to learn what is good and to despise the evil, and offer your prayers to the Almighty God and rely on Him alone, and by His blessing you may continue to improve your time well. You can have no idea how the people here are devoted to the Virgin Mary. At every corner of the streets there is the image of her, and some of these have lights burning day and night. I think of you very often: perhaps I shall never have the pleasure of seeing you again. I have been unwell ever since I came to this country. However, I am yet able to attend my school and studies. I hope I will not be worse, so that I may be unable to follow my intention.

There are really fine things to be seen in Rome. On the feast of SS. Sebastian and Fabian we visited the Catacombs, two or three miles out of the city, where is a church dedicated to those saints, which I have already mentioned in previous letters. Perhaps our countrymen would not believe that there was such a place as that place which I saw myself with my own naked eyes. We entered in with lights and saw the scene before us. As soon as we entered we saw coffins on the top of each other, in one of which we saw some of the remains. The cave runs in every direction, sometimes is ascended by steps, and sometimes runs deeper, and one would be very easily lost in it. There are some large places and a chapel; I am told by the students that the chapel is where Pope Gregory was accustomed to say mass. I assure you it would excite any human heart to behold the place where the ancient Christians were concealed under the earth from the persecution of the anti-christians. Indeed they were concealed by the power of God. They sought Jesus and Him alone they loved.

It is the custom of the College of the Propaganda, on the feast of Epiphany each year, that the students should deliver a discourse in their own respective languages. This year there were thirty-one different languages delivered by the students, so you may judge what kind of a college this is. At present it is quite full; there are ninety-three, of which thirteen are from the United States.

On Easter Sunday the Holy Father celebrated mass in the church of St. Peter. It is very seldom that his holiness is seen personally celebrating mass in public except on great festivals. The church was crowded with spectators, both citizens of Rome and foreigners. On the front part of the church there was an elevated place beautifully ornamented. After the solemn ceremonies the Holy Father went up and gave his paternal benediction to the people. There is a large square before St. Peter's, and it was crowded so that it was impossible to kneel down to receive the benediction.

This week we are quite merry; we seem to employ our minds on the merriment which is always displayed amongst us on such occasions. Our secretary is now Cardinal, and to-morrow he will be crowned with the dignity of the Cardinal. Our college has been illuminated these two evenings. The congregational halls of the Propaganda were opened on this occasion. The new Cardinal then received all the compliments of the Cardinals, Bishops, Prelates, Ambassadors, Princes, and other distinguished dignities. There are two large beautiful rooms, in one of which the new Cardinal was seated and received all those who came to pay him compliments. The visitors all came through the same passage, and there was a man posted in each room who received them and cried out to others that such man was coming, and so on through all those that were placed for the purpose, and one called the Cardinal gentleman introduced them to the new Cardinal. If there were such a thing in America it would be quite a novelty.

It is time for me to close, and I hope you will write me sometimes. My respects to the Sisters and Father Mullen. Farewell, dear sister; pray for your Superior and for me.

I remain your most affectionate brother,

WILLIAM MACCATEBINESSI.

After his death, some one at Cincinnati wrote the following, to be repeated before a large audience in that city by his little sister Margaret, who was there at school. The poetry was impressively recited and listened to by many people with wet eyes. This gifted child of nature died June 25, 1833.

"The morning breaks; see how the glorious sun,
Slow wheeling from the east, new lustre sheds
O'er the soft clime of Italy. The flower
That kept its perfume in the dewy night,

Now breathes it forth again. Hill, vale and grove,
Clad in rich verdure, bloom, and from the rocks
The joyous waters leap. O! meet it is
That thou, imperial Rome, should lift thy head,
Decked with the triple crown, where cloudless skies
And lands rejoicing in the summer sun,
Rich blessings yield.

But there is grief to-day.
A voice is heard within thy marble walls,
A voice lamenting for the youthful dead;
For o'er the relics of her forest boy
The mother of dead Empires weeps. And lo!
Clad in white robes the long procession moves;
Youths throng around the bier, and high in front,
Star of our hope, the glorious cross is reared,
Triumphant sign. The low, sweet voice of prayer,
Flowing spontaneous from the spirit's depths,
Pours its rich tones; and now the requiem swells,
Now dies upon the ear.

But there is one*
Who stands beside my brother's grave, and tho' no tear
Dims his dark eye, yet does his spirit weep.
With beating heart he gazes on the spot
Where his young comrade shall forever rest.
For they together left their forest home,
Led by Father Reese, who to their fathers preached
Glad tiding of great joy; the holy man my brother,
Who sleeps beneath the soil the Father Reese's labors blessed.
How must the spirit mourn, the bosom heave,
Of that lone Indian boy! No tongue can speak
The accents of his tribe, and as he bends
In melancholy mood above the dead,

*His cousin Hamlin.

Imagination clothes his tearful thoughts
In rude but plaintive cadences.

Soft be my brother's sleep!
At nature's call the cypress here shall wave,
The wailing winds lament above the grave,
The dewy night shall weep.

And he thou leavest forlorn,
Oh, he shall come to shade my brother's grave with moss,
To plant what thou didst love—the mystic cross,
To hope, to pray, to mourn.

No marble here shall rise;
But o'er thy grave he'll teach the forest tree
To lift its glorious head and point to thee,
Rejoicing in the skies.

And when it feels the breeze,
I'll think thy spirit wakes that gentle sound
Such as our fathers thought when all around
Shook the old forest leaves.

Dost thou forget the hour, my brother,
When first we heard the Christian's hope revealed,
When fearless warriors felt their bosoms yield
Beneath Almighty power?

Then truths came o'er us fast,
Whilst on the mound the missionary stood
And thro' the list'ning silence of the wood
His words like spirits passed.

And oh, hadst thou been spared,
We two had gone to bless our fathers' land,
To spread rich stores around, and hand in hand
Each holy labor shared.

But here the relics of my brother lie,
Where nature's flowers shall bloom o'er nature's child,
Where ruins stretch, and classic art has piled
Her monuments on high.

Sleep on, my brother, sleep peaceful here
The traveler from thy land will claim this spot,
And give to thee what kingly tombs have not—
The tribute of a tear with me, my brother.

He died almost the very day when he was to be ordained a priest. He received a long visit from his cousin Hamlin that evening, and they sat late in the night, talking on various subjects, and particularly on American matters and his ordination. My brother was perfectly well and robust at that time, and full of lively spirits. He told his cousin that night, that if he ever set his foot again on American soil, his people, the Ottawas and Chippewas of Michigan, should always remain where they were. The United States would never be able to compel them to go west of the Mississippi, for he knew the way to prevent them from being driven off from their native land. He also told his cousin that as soon as he was ordained and relieved from Rome, he would at once start for America, and go right straight to Washington to see the President of the United States, in order to hold conference with him on the subject of his people and their lands. There was a great preparation for the occasion of his ordination. A great cermony was to be in St. Peter's Church, because a native American Indian, son of the chief of the Ottawa tribe of Indians, a prince of the forests of Michigan, was to be ordained a priest, which had never before happened since the discovery of the Aborigines in America. In the morning, at the breakfast table, my brother William did not appear, and every one was surprised not to see him at the table. After breaklast, a messenger was sent to his room. He soon returned with the shocking news that he was dead. Then the authorities of the college arose and rushed to the scene, and there they found him on the floor, lying in his own blood. When Hamlin, his cousin heard of it, he too rushed to the room; and after his cousin's body was taken out, wrapped up in a cloth, he went in, and saw at once enough to tell him that it was the work of the assassin.

When the news reached to Little Traverse, now Harbor Springs, all the country of Arbor Croche was enveloped in deep mourning, and a great lamentation took place among the Ottawas and Chippewas in this country with the expression, "All our hope is gone." Many people came to our dwelling to learn full particulars of my brother's death, and to console and mourn with his father in his great bereavement.

No motive for the assassination has ever been developed, and it remains to this day a mystery. It was related that there was no known enemy in the institution previous to his death, but he was much thought of and beloved by every one in the college. It was an honor to be with him and to converse with him, as it is related that his conversation was always most noble and instructive. It was even considered a great honor to sit by him at the tables; as it is related that the students of the college used to have a strife amongst themselves who should be the first to sit by him. There were several American students at Rome at that time, and it was claimed by the Italians that my brother's death came through some of the American students from a secret plot originating in this country to remove this Indian youth who had attained the highest pinnacle of science and who had become their equal in wisdom, and in all the important questions of the day, both in temporal and spiritual matters. He was slain, it has been said, because it was found out that he was counseling his people on the subject of their lands and their treaties with the Government of the United States. His death deprived the Ottawa and Chippewa Indians of a wise counselor and adviser, one of their [illegible]tive countrymen; but it seems that it would be impossible [illegible] American people in this Christian land to make such a wicked conspiracy against this poor son of the forest who had become as wise as any of them and a great statesman for his country. Yet it might be possible, for we have learned that we cannot always trust the American people as to their integrity and stability in well doing with us.

It is said the stains of my brother's blood can be seen to this day in Rome, as the room has been kept as a memorial, and is shown to travelers from this country. His statue in full size can also be seen there, which is said to be a perfect image of him. His trunk containing his books and clothing was sent from Rome to this country, and it came all right until it reached Detroit. There it was lost, or exchanged for another, which was sent to Little Traverse. It was sent back with a request to forward the right one, but that was the end of it, and no explanation was ever received.

Soon after the death of my brother William, my sister Margaret left Cincinnati, Ohio, and came to Detroit, Mich., where she was employed as teacher of the orphan children at a Catholic institution. She left Detroit about 1835, and came to Little Traverse, where she at once began to teach the Indian children for the Catholic mission. She has ever since been very useful to her people, but is now a decrepit old lady and sometimes goes by the name of Aunty Margaret, or Queen of the Ottawas. She is constantly employed in making Indian curiosities—wearing out her fingers and eyes to make her living and keep her home. Like many others of her race, she has been made the victim of fraud and extortion. Some years ago a white man came to the Indian country and committed many crimes, for some of which he is now in prison. Soon after he came here, this wicked man pretended he was gored by an ox—although there were no marks of of violence—which he claimed belonged to Mr. Boyd, Aunty Margaret's husband, and he therefore sued Mr. Boyd for damages for several hundred dollars; and although the ox which he claimed had injured him did not belong to Mr. Boyd, and there was no eye witness in the case, yet he obtained judgment for damages against him, and a mortgage had to be given on the land which the Government had given her. The Indian's oath and evidence are not regarded in this country, and he stands a very poor chance before the law. Although they are citizens of the State, they are continually being taken advantage of by the attorneys of the land; they are continually being robbed and cheated out of their property, and they can obtain no protection nor redress whatever.

Before Mr. Hamlin, my cousin, left Italy, he was asked by the authorities if William had any younger brother in America of a fit age to attend school. He told the authorities that the deceased had one brother just the right age to begin school--that was myself. Then there was an order for me to be sent to Rome to take the place of my brother; but when my father heard of it, he said, "No; they have killed one of my sons after they have educated him, and they will kill another." Hamlin came home soon after my brother's death, and some time after the Treaty of 1836 he was appointed U. S. Interpreter and continued to hold this office until 1861, at which time I succeeded him.

CHAPTER VI.

Account of the Indians' Roving Disposition, Their Feasts and Their Customs—Saluting Arbor Croche Every Spring of the Year—How the Catholic Religion was Introduced Among the Ottawas—The Missions—Signing of the Treaty, March 8, 1836.

I will again return to my narrative respecting how the Ottawas used to live and travel to and fro in the State of Michigan, and how they came to join the Catholic religion at Arbor Croche. Early in the spring we used to come down this beautiful stream of water (Muskegon River) in our long bark canoes, loaded with sugar, furs, deer skins, prepared venison for summer use, bear's oil, and bear meat prepared in oil, deer tallow, and sometimes a lot of honey, etc. On reaching the mouth of this river we halted for five or six days, when all the other Indians gathered, as was customary, expressly to feast for the dead. All the Indians and children used to go around among the camps and salute one another with the words, "Ne-baw-baw-tche-baw-yew," that is to say, "I am or we are going around as spirits," feasting and throwing food into the fire—as they believe the spirits of the dead take the victuals and eat as they are consumed in the fire.

After the feast of the dead, we would all start for Arbor Croche, our summer resort, to plant our corn and other vegetables. At the crossing of Little Traverse Bay at the point called "Ki-tche-ossening," that is to say, "on the big rock," all the Indians waited until all the canoes arrived, after which they would all start together in crossing the bay. When about half way across they would begin to salute Arbor Croche by shooting with guns, holding them close to the water in order that the sound might reach to each side of the bay, to be heard by those few who always made their winter quarters around Little Traverse Bay. Arriving at Arbor Croche, where our big wigwam would be waiting for us—of which I have spoken in previous chapters—the very first thing my parents would do would be to go and examine their stores of corn and beans. After all the Indians arrived and had settled down, they would again have a prolonged merriment and another feasting of the dead and peace offerings. Grand medicine dances, fire dances, and many other jubilant performances my people would have before they would go to work again to plant their corn. I distinctly remember the time, and I have seen my brothers and myself dancing around the fires in our great wigwam, which had two fireplaces inside of it.

About in 1824, there was an Indian came from Montreal whose name was Andowish, and who formerly belonged to Arbor Croche. He was among the Stockbridge Indians somewhere near Montreal, and this tribe speak a dialect of the Ottawa and Chippewa languages, and most of them by this time had joined the Catholic church. So Andowish, by their influence, also joined the Catholic religion out there with the Stockbridge Indians. Coming back to Arbor Croche, where he formerly belonged, he began to teach some of his own relatives the faith of the Catholic religion, which some of them were very ready to receive, but he could not baptize them. Therefore, parties of Indians went to Mackinac Island, headed by the principal chief of the Seven Mile Point band of Indians, whose name was A-paw-kau-se-gun, to see some of their half-breed relations at the island, relating to them how they felt with regard to Christianity, and asking advice as to what they should do in the matter. These half-breed relatives promised they would do all they could to cause the priest to come up to Arbor Croche and baptize all those Indians who felt disposed to receive the religion. Therefore in 1825 Rev. Father Baden, an old priest, came up with his interpreters and landed at Seven Mile Point, and baptized quite a number of grown folks, and a great many children were taken into the Catholic religion. At this time, I was also baptized by Rev. Father Baden; I was small, but I distinctly remember having the water poured over my head and putting some salt in my mouth, and changing my name from Pe-ness-wi-qua-am to Amable. The mission was then established at Seven Mile Point, where a church was built with poles and covered with cedar bark. This was the very way that the first religion was introduced among the Ottawas, although everybody supposes that some white people or missionary societies brought the Christian religion among the Ottawa tribes of Indians at Arbor Croche.

My uncle, Au-se-go-nock, had before this joined the Catholic religion. He was living at that time at Drummond's Island with the British people, where all the Ottawas and Chippewas used to go every summer to receive presents from the British Government. And when he learned that his people had joined the Catholic faith, he left his home at Drummond's Island and came to Arbor Croche expressly to act as missionary in the absence of the priest. Every Sunday he preached to his people and taught them how to pray to God and to the Virgin Mary and all the saints and angels in heaven. At that time printed books containing prayers and hymns in the Stockbridge Indian language, which is a dialect of the Ottawa and Chippewa languages, were brought from Montreal, and could be quite intelligently understood by the Ottawas. By this time many Indians began to be stationary; they did not go south, as heretofore, but remained and made their winter quarters ar Arbor Croche.

About 1827, after several councils, it was determined to remove the Mission from Seven Mile Point to Little Traverse, and a French priest whose name was Dejan arrived expressly to remain there and carry on the new mission established at Little Traverse. A log church was built at the new mission, which stood very near where the present church is now standing, and a log school house was built just where the Star Hotel now stands, and also a log house for the priest to live in, which is standing to this day nearest the church, but it has been covered with siding boards since. In the fall of 1827, my father left his subjects at Arbor

Croche proper, now Middle Village, in charge of his brother, Kaw-me-no-te-a, which means Good-heart, as he was persuaded by other chiefs to come and establish himself where the mission was and send his children to school. There were only three Indian log houses at that time in Little Traverse, one belonging to my uncle, Au-se-ge-nock, one for Joseph Au-saw-gon, my father's messenger, and another to Peter Sho-min. But we and all other Indians lived in wigwams, and all the Indians were dressed in Indian style. Rev. Mr. Dejan brought with him one Frenchman from Detroit named Joseph Letorenue as school teacher, and two girls from Mackinac Island as domestic servants, and an old nun, whose real name I never learned, and knew only as "Sister." She was exceedingly kind to Indian children and we all liked her very much. The log school house was used as a dwelling as well as a school house, as all the boys and girls who attended school were kept there continually, same as boarding school. The larger boys and girls were taught household duties and to cook for the scholars. The children were kept quite clean. The French teacher took very great pains to teach them good manners, and they were taught no other but the French language. In the spring of the year each family of Indians contributed one large mocok* of sugar which weighed from eighty to one hundred pounds, which Priest Dejan would empty into barrels, and then go down to Detroit with it to buy dry goods, returning with cloth with which to clothe his Indian children. Rev. Mr. Dejan did not say mass on week days, only on Sundays. He visited the Indians a good deal during the week days, purposely to instruct them in the manners and customs of the white man, ordering things generally how to be done, and how the women should do towards their domestic callings, not to work out of doors, and to take good care of what belonged to their household. Mr. Dejan was a great friend of Col. Boyd, Indian Agent at Mackinac, and in the

* A kind of box made of birch bark.

second year of the school, Mr. Boyd's two sons, James and George, wintered with the priest at the mission, and were very great friends to the Indians.

In two years schooling the children progressed very much, both in reading the French language, and in learning the manners and customs of the white man. But, alas, this was carried on only two years. There was some trouble between Rev. Mr. Dejan and Bishop Reese of Detroit, consequently Mr. Dejan was removed from the mission, and Rev. Mr. Baraga was put in instead in the year 1830. He promised to do the same as his predecessor in regard to carrying on the Indian school at Little Traverse; but he did not. He did not give as good care to the children as his predecessor, and he did not teach them anything but Indian and the catechism. He, however, made and published a prayer book in the Ottawa language and a short Bible History. Before two years the boarding school was out of existence at Little Traverse, and Mr. Baraga went away to Lake Superior, where some time afterwards he was made Bishop. After he was in the Lake Superior country he published some more books, such as Odjebwe dictionary and Odjebwe grammar, which were very hard to understand to one unacquainted with the Indian language, and he also made a new catechism. Father Simon succeeded Mr. Baraga, and did about the same thing with regard to educating the Indian youths, as did also Father Pierce after Simon, and many others from time to time up to this day.

The Indians were very strict in their religion at this time They did not allow any drunkenness in their village, nor allow any one to bring intoxicating liquors within the Harbor. If any person, white or Indian, brought any liquor into the Harbor, by the barrel or in small quantities, and it came to the knowledge of the old chief, Au-paw-ko-si-gan, who was the war chief, but was acting as principal chief at Little Traverse, he would call out his men to go and search for the liquor, and if found he would order him men to spill the whisky on the ground by knocking the head of a barrel with an ax, telling them not to bring any more whisky into the Harbor, or wherever the Ottawas are, along the coast of Arbor Croche. This was the end of it, there being no law suit for the whisky.

They used to observe many holidays, particularly Christmas, New Years and Corpus Christi. At the New Year's eve, every one of the Indians used to go around visiting the principal men of the tribe, shooting their guns close to their doors after screaming three times, "Happy New Year," then bang, bang, altogether, blowing their tin horns and beating their drums, etc. Early on the New Year's morning, they would go around among their neighbors expressly to shake hands one with another, with the words of salutation, "Bozhoo," children and all. This practice was kept up for a long time, or until the white people came and intermingled with the tribes.

I thought my people were very happy in those days, when they were all by themselves and possessed a wide spread of land, and no one to quarrel with them as to where they should make their gardens, or take timber, or make sugar. And fishes of all kinds were so plentiful in the Harbor. A hook anywheres in the bay, and at any time of the year, would catch Mackinaw trout, many as one would want. And if a net were set anywheres in the harbor on shallow water, in the morning it would be loaded with fishes of all kinds. Truly this was a beautiful location for the mission. Every big council of the Indians was transacted in the village of Little Traverse.

I will mention one or two more things which it might be interesting to my readers to know. Up to 1835 and some time afterwards, there was a very large double cedar tree, which appeared to have been stuck together while they were growing, but were two separate trees of the same size and height growing very close together, standing very near the edge of the water, and leaning very much towards the bay, almost like a staircase projecting far out into the bay. Under the roots of these trees issued a perpetual spring of water, which is now called Mr. Carlow's Spring, near the present depot. In the fall of 1835, I was clear at the top of those trees, with my little chums, watching our people as they were about going off in a long bark canoe, and, as we understood, they were going to Washington to see the Great Father, the President of the United States, to tell him to have mercy on the Ottawa and Chippewa Indians in Michigan, not to take all the land away from them. I saw some of our old Indian women weeping as they watched our principal men going off in the canoe. I suppose they were feeling bad on account of not knowing their future destinies respecting their possession of the land. After they all got in the canoe, just as they were going to start, they all took off their hats, crossed themselves and repeated the Lord's prayer; at the end of the prayer, they crossed themselves again, and then away they went towards the Harbor Point. We watched them until they disappeared in rounding the point.

March 28th, 1836, a treaty was signed at Washington, not with the free will of the Indians, but by compulsion. That same year we received the first annuity at Mackinac Island, our trading post, $10 cash per head, beside dry goods and provisions. There was a stipulation expressed in the 7th clause of the 4th article of said treaty, that there was to be given to the Ottawa and Chippewa Indians of Michigan $150,000 worth of dry goods until all was paid out. There is said to have been paid out on the first payment in 1836, about $10,000, which would then leave a balance of $140,000. At this time the Ottawas and Chippewas held a big council and concluded to ask the Government for cash instead of dry goods; because they saw that there was a great deal of waste in distributing the goods among them, as there were lots of remnants, and much of it left after distribution which they never knew what became of. Therefore their belief respecting it was that the Government officials had appropriated to themselves some of these dry goods and given away freely to their white friends and relatives. After conclusion of the council, they came before the Indian agent, Hon. H. Schoolcraft, and presented their views and their request in this matter. He told them that he could not give them any conclusive reply upon this subject, but that he would make known their wishes to their Great Father at Washington, and would inform them thereafter. That was the last of it. In the next payment there were neither goods nor money instead, as they requested, and no reply ever came to this day. It was also stipulated that at the expiration of twenty-one years, $20,000 was to be given to the Ottawa and Chippewa Indians, that is, one year after the expiration of the payment of their annuities. And where are those lawful promises gone to now? Alas! when we inquire of them to the head department they refer us to the third article of the Treaty of 1855, where it is worded, "That the Ottawa and Chippewa Indians hereby release and discharge the United States from all liability on account of former treaty stipulations, either land or money," etc. But this part of the stipulation was never explained to them at the Council of Detroit, as they would never have consented to it, and would not have signed the contract. We did not know anything about it, but some time after we saw it with our own eyes, printed in the pamphlet form of the contract, where our names had been already subscribed to it. Then it was too late to make any remedy in the matter.

CHAPTER VII.

More Personal History—Suffering and Trials in Early Life—Missing the Opportunity to Go to School—Learning Trade as a Blacksmith—A New Start to Seek for Education—Arriving at Cleveland, O., to Find His Old Friend, Rev. Alvin Coe—Visit with Rev. Samuel Bissell, of Twinsburg, O., Principal of the Twinsburg Institute—Attending School—Returning Home—Advocating Citizenship for His People—Delegated to Detroit and to the State Legislature—His Pleasant Visit with State Authorities—Again Delegated as Councilor to the New Treaty, 1855.

The first winter we lived at Little Traverse as a permanent home was in the year 1828, and in the following spring my own dear mother died very suddenly, as she was burned while they were making sugar in the woods. She was burned so badly that she only lived four days after. I was small, but I was old enough to know and mourn for my dear mother. I felt as though I had lost everything dear to me and every friend; there was no one that I could place such confidence in, not even my own father. So my father's household was broken up: we were pretty well scattered after that. He could not very well keep us together; being the least one in the family, I became a perfect wild rover. At last I left Little Traverse when about 13 or 14 years age. I went to Green Bay, Wis., with the expectation of living with an older sister who had married a Scotchman named Gibson and had gone there to make a home somewhere in Green Bay. I found them, but I did not stay with them long. I left them and went to live with a farmer close by whose name was Sylvester. From this place I was persuaded by another man to go with him on the fishing ground, to a place called Sturgeon Bay, Wis. From there I sailed with Mr. Robert Campbell. Mr. Campbell was a good man and Christian. His father had a nice farm at Bay Settlement, near Green Bay, Wis., where also my sister settled down. I sailed with him one summer. We came to Mackinac Island in the fall of 1840, and there I met my father and all my relations, and great many Indians as they were about receiving their annual payment from the Government. So I left the vessel and hired out in the store to act as clerk during the payment time.

After all the Indians had gone away from the island, I was still working in the store and thought to make my winter quarters there, but did not. One day I met my father's old friend, the Rev. Mr. Alvin Coe, the traveling missionary of whom I have already spoken as having asked me to go with him to the State of Ohio where I might have an opportunity to go to school and be educated like the white man. I told him I will go with him, provided he will take an interest to watch over me, that no one would abuse me out there after getting into the strange country. He faithfully promised that he wonld do all this, and would also do all he could to help me along to obtain my education. He said he was going that night and I must be on hand when the boat arrived; but I failed to tell him my stopping place. So when the boat arrived I was too sound asleep to hear it. Poor old man! I was told that he felt disappointed to have to go without me. As I woke in the morning I inquired if any boat had arrived during the night. I was told there was. I was also told there was an old man who seemed to be very anxious, and was looking for me all over the crowd on the dock, but he could not find me there. When the boat was pushing out he jumped on board and then turned to the crowd, saying, "Tell my little boy, Jackson, son of the old chief Macka-de-be-nessy, of Arbor Croche, that I have gone on this boat."

Thus I was left, and missed the opportunity when I might have been educated while I was yet much younger. A few days afterwards, as I walked out from the store one evening, I met two young men in the street, one of whom I frequently saw during the payment time, but the other was entirely a stranger to me.

He was a most noble-looking and tall young man, but, behold, he spoke perfectly and freely the Indian language, saying to me, "My boy, would you be willing to take us to that vessel out there?" at the same time pointing to a vessel which was already outside of the harbor, sails up, but in a perfectly dead calm, as there was not a breath of wind. I told them I would, provided I could get the boat to get there; in which he replied that they will do all that part of the business, but they wanted some one to bring the boat back. As I was walking with another mate of mine, I ask him to go with me to take these folks on board. The next thing we were on the way towards the vessel. As we went along this noble young man said to me, "My boy, would you like to come with us to Grand Traverse?" I replied, "I would like to see Grand Traverse, but am not prepared to go just now." "Would you not like to learn the blacksmith trade? This man is a government blacksmith in Grand Traverse," referring to his companion, "and he needs an assistant in the business. We will give you position as an assistant and a salary of $240 yearly, or $20 per month." I replied, "I will go, for I would be very glad to find a chance to learn a trade and at the same time to get my living." Therefore I also got on board, and my friend had to come back alone with the boat we borrowed. This was the same vessel that I had sailed on that season. We arrived at the place now called "The Old Mission," where there was a nice harbor.* This young man, whose name I now learned was John M. Johnstone, of Sault Ste. Marie, the brother-in-law of Henry Schoolcraft, our Indian agent, said when we arrived, "You have no commission yet to work in the shop; you will therefore have to go back to Mackinac with

* The Mission was already established by this time, 1840, conducted by the Presbyterian Board of Missions. Rev. P. Dougherty, who was indeed a true Christian, and good to Indians, was a preacher for the Mission. Daniel Rod, the half-breed from St. Clair River, Mich., was his interpreter. Mr. Bradley acted as teacher, who afterwards proved himself unworthy for the position, which produced a bad effect among the Indians. The Mission is now out of existence.

this letter which you will take to Indian agent yourself and nobody else. Then come back at the first opportunity if he tells you to come."

So I had to return to Mackinac on the same vessel with which we went away. At Mackinac I received my commission without any trouble. On arriving at Grand Traverse the Indians were having a big council which was concocted, I was told, by the brother of my benefactor, who was trading there among the Indians. They were getting up remonstrances and petitioning the Government against my appointment, setting forth as reason of their complaint that I did not belong to that tribe of Indians, and was therefore not entitled to the position, and they would rather have one of their own boys belonging to the tribe put to this trade. But my friend Johnstone told me "not to mind anything, but go about my business. The blacksmith shop had been established here for more than two years, and they should have thought of putting their boy in the shop long before this." So accordingly I continued working and minding my own business for five years, when I quit of my own accord. There were no white people there at that time, only such as were employed by the Government, and the missionaries and teachers, and the Indians were very happy in those days.

I have told my readers in the previous chapters of this little book, that from the time I was invited by our most estimable friend, Rev. Alvin Coe, to go with him to the State of Ohio in order to receive an education, "that it was never blotted out of my mind," and therefore the very day I quit the blacksmith shop at Grand Traverse, I turned my face toward the State of Ohio, for that object alone. I came to Little Traverse to bid a good-by to my father and relations late in October, 1845. I did not even stay half a day at Little Traverse. I started for Arbor Croche the same day I bid the last farewell to my folks, in order to obtain an opportunity there to get to Mackinac Island, from which I intended to take my passage for Cleveland. Arriving at Arbor

Croche, which is fourteen miles from Little Traverse, I met an orphan boy, Paul Naw-o-ga-de by name, a distant relative, and proposed to pay his passage to Cleveland. The brother of this little boy had a boat of his own, and offered to take us to Mackinac Island, and I was vary glad of the opportunity. So the next day we started for Mackinac, not knowing what would become of us if my little means were exhausted and we should be unsuccessful in finding our old friend, Mr. Alvin Coe.

The day we arrived at Mackinac we took passage for Cleveland. Arriving there we were scared at seeing so many people coming to us who wanted us to get into their cabs to take us to some hotel which might cost us two or three dollars a day. We went to Farmer's Hotel. In the evening the landlady was somewhat curious to know where we hailed from and where we were going to. I told her we came from Michigan, but we did not know yet where we should go to. I asked her if she ever knew or heard of a minister named Alvin Coe. "What,"—she seemed to be very much surprised—"Mr. Alvin Coe the traveling missionary?" I said, "Yes, the same." "Why, that is my own uncle. What is it about him?" "O, nothing; only I would like to know where he lives, and how far." I was equally surprised to think that we happened to meet one of his relatives, and thought at this moment, God must be with us in our undertaking. "You know my uncle, then," she said. I said, "Yes; he is my particular friend, and I am going to look for him." Of course, she told us the name of the town in which he lived, and how far and which road to take to get there. It also happened that there was one gentleman at Farmer's Hotel, who had been out west and came on the same boat on which we came, and he was going the next day in that direction on foot, and said he would guide us as far as he would go, which would be about twenty miles, and there was thirty miles to go after that. So the next day we started. Arriving late in the afternoon at the outskirts of the little village called Twinsburg, our white companion told us this is the place where he intended to stop for a while, and said, "You better stop with me for the night, and after supper you could visit the institution in the village and see the principal of the school here; you might possibly get a chance to attend that school, as you say that was your object in coming to this part of the country." I was very much surprised, as he had not said one word about it as we came along on the road. After supper, I went as he directed. As I approached the seminary I saw a good many boys playing on the square of the village, and I went and stood close by. Very soon one of the young men came up to me, saying, "Are you going to attend our school here?" I told him, "No, sir; I am going thirty miles further to attend some school there." "This is the best school that I know of anywhere about this country," he said. I asked him if he would introduce me to the proprietor of the school. "Most cheerfully," said he; "will you please to tell me what place you came from, and your name." "I came from Michigan, and my name is Blackbird." "All right, I will go with you." So we came to the professor's room, and he introduced me. "Well, Mr. Blackbird, do you wish to attend our school?" I said, "I do not know, sir, how that might be, as I have not much means to pay my way, but I am seeking for a man who invited me to come to come to Ohio some five years ago, and promised that he would help me all he could for my education. His name is Alvin Coe, a traveling missionary, my father's old friend." "We have two Indian boys here attending school, and I think you will not be very lonesome if you should conclude to stay with us." "What are their names?" I asked. "One is Francis Petoskey, and the other is Paul Ka-gwe-tosóng." I said, "I know them both; I came from the same place they did, but I did not know they were here, I only knew they were attending school somewhere among the whites." "Can you do any kind of work?" "I am a blacksmith by trade, sir, and besides I can do most every other kind of work." He said, "If you conclude to stay, I will try to aid you in finding a place where you could work to pay for your lodging and board; and in the meantime we will cause Mr. Alvin Coe to come and see you, and if he sees fit to take you away he can do so, provided you would be willing to go with him." I told him I would stay, if I found a place to work to pay for my board, and provided that I could make some arrangement for the little companion who came with me. After considering a few moments, he proposed to take my little companion to his boarding house until a better arrangment could be made. This was the end of my conversation with this noble hearted professor and proprietor of this Institution, whose name was Rev. Samuel Bissell, of Twinsburg, Ohio.

In the morning, after breakfast, I went back to the village and found arrangments were already made for both of us, and all we had to do was just to shift our quarters. I came to live with a young blacksmith in the village and work two hours in the morning and two hours in the evening, and many times I finished my hours at sunrise. Some time during the winter, my friend Mr. Alvin Coe came and took me off, with the understanding, however, that if I did not like the school where he was, I was to come back to Twinsburg. So in about two weeks I came back to the old institution, as I did not like the place. At last Dr. Brainsmade, of Newark, New Jersey, took a deep interest in my welfare and education, and he proposed to aid me and take me through the medical college. Therefore I quit working my hours in the shop and boarded at the institution, attending solely to my studies for over four years.

I have already told my readers in previous chapters how bad I felt when I had to return to Michigan. After I came home I did everything towards the welfare and happiness of my people, beside attending to my aged father, as I found my people to be very different then from what they were, as they were beginning to have a free use of intoxicating liquors. I immediately caused the pledge to be signed in every village of the Indians, in which I was quite successful, as almost everyone pledged themselves never again to touch intoxicating drinks. I also advocated the right of citizenship for my people in the State of Michigan, although we were repeatedly told by our white neighbors that we could not very well be adopted as citizens of the State as long as we were receiving annuities from the general government on account of our former treaties. My object of promulgating this cause was, I thought it would be the only salvation of my people from being sent off to the west of the Mississippi, where perhaps, more than one-half would have died before they could be acclimated to the country to which they would be driven. I have suffered very great hardships for this cause, as I had to walk from Little Traverse through the dense forest, and almost the entire length of the southern peninsula of Michigan, in order to reach the authorities of the State to hold conference with them upon the subject of the citizenship of the Ottawas and Chippewas, and walked on snow-shoes in the middle of winter in company with one of our young chieftains from Cross Village.* We were subjected to great exposure with only a camp fire for several days in the month of February.

After crossing Houghton Lake, which is the head waters of the Muskegon river, that evening we swallowed the last morsel of food, and actually we traveled and camped out with empty stomachs for two days and a half before we came to any inhabited place. At last we struck the Te-ti-pe-wa-say (Tittabawassee), one of the principal branches of Saginaw river, and following down that stream on the ice we came to an Indian camp which stood by the river side, and also saw many human foot-prints on the ice, but the camp was deserted and we found nothing to eat. We left the place and once more followed the river, and after walking about half a mile we came to another Indian camp, and saw blue smoke coming out of it. As we came up to the camp we found

* Mr. Wardsworth also accompanied us from Elk Rapids, on his way to Detroit to obtain a commission as surveyor on some part of the Grand Traverse region.

nothing but women and children (all the men were out hunting). They gave us food, and we went on our journey the next day.

We went to Detroit to see Judge Wing to obtain his legal opinion on the subject of the citizenship of the Ottawa and Chippewa Indians of Michigan. We had a very pleasant visit with him, and he gave us as his legal opinion of this matter, that he did not think that it would debar us from being citizens of the State, because the Government owed us a little money on account of our former treaties, provided we should renounce our allegiance to our chiefs. and recognize no other chief authority than the President of the United States; and that we would not be required to have any writ of naturalization as we are already naturalized by being American born. After a pleasant visit with Hon. Judge Wing, we next turned our faces to the State Legislature and Governor. In this also we thought we were very successful, for the Governor received us very kindly and gave us much good counsel on the subject of citizenship, giving us some instructions as to how we should live under the rule of the State if we should become the children of the same. He talked to us as though he was talking to his own son who had just come from a far country and asked his father's permission to stay in the household.

After a pleasant visit with the Governor, and seeing some of the members of the State Legislature, receiving full assurance that our undertaking and object would be well looked after, we retraced our steps back to Little Traverse, to report the result of our visit. After that, not many Indians believed these flying reports gotten up by our white neighbors. In that year, the clause was put in the revised statutes of the State of Michigan, that every male person of Indian descent in Michigan not members of any tribe shall be entitled to vote.

In the year 1855, I was again delegated to attend the council of Detroit for the treaty of 1855, and in that council I made several speeches before the Hon. Commissioner of Indian Affairs, Mr.

Manypenny, of Washington, on the subject of our educational fund, $8000 per annum, which had been expended for the education of the Indian youths for the last nineteen years, and which was to be continued ten years longer. This sum had never been used directly for any scholars, but it was stated that it was given to the religious societies which had missions among the Michigan Indians. In that council I advocated that the said fund be retained in the hands of the general Government for the benefit of those Indian youths who really intended to be educated and who went among the whites or in civilized communities to be educated, and if it need be, to be used for the collegiate education of those Indian youths, but let the children at home be educated at home by taxation, and giving fully my reasons in advancing such proposition. The Hon. Commissioner was much taken up with my remarks on this subject, I being the youngest member, and told the older members of the council that he would like to hear some of them on this subject. "The young man who has been making remarks on this matter has a very good idea with regard to your educational funds; now let us hear farther remarks on this subject by some other members of the council." But not one Indian stirred. And again and again the next day, I tried to urge this matter to the Hon. Commissioner and the Indians to coöperate with me, but they would not, because my people were so ignorant they did not know the value of education, or else they misunderstood the whole subject. On the third day, as I was about getting up to make further remarks upon this subject, one of the old members, who was the most unworthy of all the company, as he got very drunk the day we arrived in Detroit and was locked up in jail as disorderly two or three days, arose and said to the Commissioner that I was not authorized by any of the council to get up here and make such remarks. "We did not come here to talk about education, but came expressly to form a treaty." Then burst into a great laughter all the spectators of the council and some of the members too. I was told afterwards that it was a put up job to prevent any change by the persons who had been handling for years this Indian educational fund, as there were a number of them in the council hall. Thus was lost one of the most noble objects which ought to have been first looked after.

After the council dispersed and came home, I sat down and and wrote a long article, giving the full history of the past in regard to this matter; how our educational fund, $8000 per annum, had been handled and conducted for nearly twenty years, and yet not one Indian youth could spell the simplest word in the English language, and these writings I had published in the Detroit Tribune for public inspection.

CHAPTER VIII.

Becoming Protestant—Persecutions—Second Attempt to go to School —Trials With Indian Agent—Governor Lewis Cass—Struggles During Education—Getting Married—Coming Home—Government Interpreter and Postmaster.

The next five years were passed among my people, doing a little of everything, laboring, teaching, and interpreting sermons among the Protestant missions—for there were by this time two Protestant missions established among the Ottawas of Arbor Croche, one at Bear River, now Petoskey, and another at Middle Village or Arbor Croche proper, where I acted as an assistant teacher and interpreter. I met much opposition from the Catholic community, because I had already become a Protestant and left the Romish church, not by any personal persuasion, however, but by terrible conviction on reading the word of God—"That there is no mediator between God and man but one, which is Christ Jesus, who was crucified for the remission of sins." One Sunday, some friend persuaded me to come to the church, but when the priest saw me he came and forcibly ejected me out of the room. The same priest left the Indian country soon afterwards, and it seems he went to England, and just before he died he wrote to my sister a very touching epistle, in which he said nothing about himself or any one in Little Traverse, but from the beginning to the end of the letter he expressed himself full of sorrow for what he had done to me when in this country among the Indians, and asking of me forgivness for his wrongs towards me.

Soon after the council of Detroit, I became very discontented, for I felt that I ought to have gone through with my medical studies, or go to some college and receive a degree and then go and study some profession. But where is the means to take me through for completing my education? was the question every day. So, after one payment of the treaty of 1855, late in the fall of 1856, I went up to Mr. Gilbert, who was then Indian agent, and made known to him my intention, and asked him if he would aid me towards completing my education, by arranging for me to receive the benefit of our educational fund, which was set apart at the last council for the education of the Indians in this State. But he would not. He bluffed me off by saying he was sorry I had voted the "black republican ticket," at the general election, which took place that fall of 1856. This was the first time that the Indians ever voted on general election. Mr. Gilbert was at North Port, Grand Traverse, on election day, managing the Indian votes there, and he sent a young man to Little Traverse to manage the voting there and sit as one of the Board at the Little Traverse election. He sent the message to Indians to vote no other ticket but the democratic ticket. At this election there were only two republican votes in Little Traverse, one of which was cast by myself. As I was depositing my ballot, this young man was so furiously enraged at me he fairly gnashed his teeth, at which I was very much surprised, and from my companion they tried to take away the ticket. Then they tried to make him exchange his ticket, but he refused. We went out quickly, as we did not wish to stay in this excitement. At that time I felt almost sorry for my people, the Indians, for ever being citizens of the State, as I thought they were much happier without these elections.

After payment of our annuities, as the vessel was about starting off to take the Indian agent to Mackinac, they had already hoisted the sails, although there was not much wind, and I thought, this was the last chance to get to Mackinac. As I looked toward the vessel I wept, for I felt terribly downcast. As they were going very slowly toward the harbor point, I asked one of the Indian youngsters to take me and my trunk in a canoe to the vessel out there. I had now determined to go, in defiance of every opposition, to seek my education.* I hurried to our house with the boy, to get my trunk and bid good bye to my aged father, and told him I was going again to some school outside, and if God permitted I hoped to return again to Little Traverse. All my father said was, "Well, my son, if you think it is best, go." And away we went. We overtook the vessel somewhere opposite Little Portage, and as I came aboard the agent's face turned red. He said, "Are you going?" I said, "Yes sir, I am going." So nothing more was said. The greater part of the night was spent by the agent and the captain gambling with cards, by which the agent lost considerable money. We arrived the next day at Mackinac, and again I approached the Indian agent with request if he could possibly arrange for me to have the benefit of our Indian educational fund, set apart for that purpose at the council of Detroit, 1855; and again he brought up the subject of my voting. Then I was beginning to feel out of humor, and I spoke rather abruptly to him, saying, "Well, sir, I now see clearly that you don't care about doing anything for my welfare because I voted for the republican party. But politics have nothing to do with my education; for the Government of the United States owes us that amount of money, not politics. I was one of the councilors when that treaty was made, and I will see some other men about this matter, sir." His face turned all purple, and as I was turning about to keep away from him, he called me back, saying, "Mr. Blackbird, how far do you intend to go to get your education?" I said, "I intend to go to Ann Arbor University, sir." "Well, I will do this much for you: I will pay your fare to Detroit. I am going by way of Chicago, but you can go down by the next boat, which will be here soon from Chicago." I thanked him, and he handed me money enough to pay my fare to Detroit.

So I reached Detroit, and went to Dr. Stuben's house and in-

*Indians are now forbidden to leave their reservations without permission from the agent, so no ambitious and determined youth can now escape from the Indian Bureau machine.—[Ed.

quired my way to Governor Cass' residence; and when I knocked at the door, behold it was he himself came to the door. I shook hands with him and said, "My friend, I would like to speak to you a few moments." "Is it for business?" he asked. "Yes sir, it is." "Well, my boy, I will listen to what you have to say." I therefore began, saying, "Well, my friend, I come from Arbor Croche. I am the nephew of your old friend, "Warrior Wing," am seeking for education, but I have no means; and I come to see you expressly to acquaint you with my object, and to ask you the favor of interceding for me to the Government to see if they could possibly do something towards defraying my expenses in this object. That is all I have to say." The old man raised his spectacles and said, "Why, why! your object is a very good one. I was well acquainted with your uncle in the frontier of Michigan during the war of 1812. Have you seen and told the Indian agent of this matter?" "Yes sir, I have asked him twice, but he would not do anything for me." "Why, why! it seems to me there is ample provision for your people for that object, and has been for the last twenty years. What is the matter with him?"

I said, "I don't know, sir." "Well, well; I am going to Washington in a few days, and shall see the Indian Commissioner about this matter, and will write to you from there on the subject. I know they can do something toward defraying your expenses. Where do you intend to go?" I said, "I don't know, yet, sir, but I thought of going to the University at Ann Arbor." "Is it possible? are you prepared to enter such a college?" I told him I thought I was. "Well, sir, I think you had better go to Ypsilanti State Normal School instead of Ann Arbor: it is one of the best colleges in the State." This was the first time I ever heard of that school, and it sounded quite big to me; so I told him that I would gladly attend that school, provided I had means to do so. "Well, then, it is settled. You shall go to Ypsilanti, and I will direct my letter to Ypsilanti when I write to you; and now mind nobody, but just go about your business." After thanking him for his good counsel I shook hands with the old man and left.

The next day was a terrible snow storm, but, however, I started out for Ypsilanti, which is only about thirty miles from Detroit. Of course, as I was totally a stranger in the place, I put up at a hotel, although my means were getting very short. The next day I went about to find out all about the institution, cost of tuition, and private board, etc., and saw some of the professors of the institution, but I did not dare to make any arrangements for a steady boarding place and begin school for fear Governor Cass should fail of getting help from the Goverment. Therefore, instead of beginning to go to school, I went and hired out on a farm about three miles from the city, and continued to work there for about three weeks before I heard from Governor Cass. At last the old farmer brought a package of letters from the post-office, one of which was post marked at Washington, D. C., and another from Detroit. I fairly trembled as I opened the one which I thought was from Governor Cass, as between doubt and hope, but my fears were suddenly changed into gladness, and quickly as possible I settled with the farmer, and away I went towards the city, singing as I went along. By intercession of Governor Cass, it was proposed to pay my whole expenses—board, clothes, books, tuition, etc. The other letter was from the Indian Agent, calling me to come down to Detroit, as he had already received some instructions from the Commissioner of Indian Affairs to look after me and to arrange the matters of my schooling at Ypsilanti State Normal School. O, how I did hate to have to meet the Indian Agent again on this subject; to stand before him, and to have him think that I had overcome him, and succeeded in spite of his opposition to my desire. O, how I wished this matter could have been arranged without his assistance. However, I started out for Detroit the same evening I received these communications, and went to the agent. He never even said, "How do you do?" but immediately began, saying,

"Well, sir, how much do you think that it will cost for your schooling at Ypsilanti?" "I don't know, sir," I responded. "Well, who knows? I think you ought to know, as you have been there," he said, in a gruff voice. "I have not been to school at all, sir," I said, "but have been working on a farm up to this morning." "Working on a farm, eh? I thought you came here on purpose to attend school?" "I did, sir; but you know I was very short of means, so I had to do something to keep me alive." "Can't you tell me the cost for your board per week?" "The private board is from $3.50 to $4 per week, sir, as according to accommodation." "How much for books and clothing?" "I don't know, sir; but I think I have enough clothing for at least one year."

In the morning I went back to Ypsilanti, and with the aid of the professors of the institution I got a good boarding place. I attended this institution almost two years and a half, when I could not hold out any longer, as my allowance for support from the Government was so scanty it did not pay for all my necessary expenses. I have always attributed this small allowance to the Indian Agent who was so much against me. I tried to board myself and to live on bread and water; and therefore hired a room which cost me 75 cents a week, and bought bread from the bakeries, which cost me about 50 cents a week, and once in a while I had fire-wood as I did not keep much fire. I stood it pretty well for three months, but I could not stand it any longer. I was very much reduced in flesh, and on the least exertion I would be trembling, and I began to be discouraged in the prosecution of my studies. By this time I was in the D class, but class F was the graduating class in that institution, which I was exceedingly anxious to attain; but I imagined that I was beginning to be sick on account of so much privation, or that I would starve to death before I could be graduated, and therefore I was forced to abandon my studies and leave the institution.

As I did not have any money to pay my passage homeward, I

went about working and occasionally lecturing on the subject of the Indians of Michigan, and at last I had enough means to return home and try to live once more according to the means and strength of my education. September 4th, 1858, I was joined in wedlock to the young lady who is still my beloved wife, and now we have four active children for whom I ever feel much anxiety that they might be educated and brought up in a Christian manner. Soon after I came to my country my father died at a great age. The first year we lived in Little Traverse we struggled quite hard to get along, but in another year I was appointed U. S. Interpreter by the Hon. D. C. Leach, U. S. Indian Agent for Mackinac Indian Agency, to whom I ever feel largely indebted, and I continued to hold this situation under several of his successors in office.

During the Rebellion I was loyal to the Government, and opposed the bad white men who were then living in the Indian country, who tried to mislead my people as to the question of the war, to cause them to be disloyal. After the war was over, I was appointed as an auxiliary prosecutor of the Indian soldier claims, as quite a number of our people also helped to pnt down this rebellion, and many were killed and wounded. But most of this kind of business I performed without reward.

Before I was fairly out as Interpreter, I was appointed with a very small salary as postmaster at Little Traverse, now Harbor Springs, where I discharged my duties faithfully and honestly for eleven years. But the ingress of the white population in this Indian country increased much from 1872-73 and onward. The office was beginning to be a paying one, and I was beginning to think that I was getting over the bridge, when others wanted the office, my opponents being the most prominent persons. Petitions were forwarded to Washington to have me removed, although no one ever had any occasion to complain of having lost his money or letter through this office during my administration. At last, the third assistant postmaster general at Washington wrote me a kind of private letter, stating that the main ground of the complaint was, that my office was too small and inconvenient for the public, and advising me to try and please the public as well as I could. And consequently I took what little money I had saved and built a comfortable office, but before the building was thoroughly completed I was removed. This left me penniless in this cold world, to battle on and to struggle for my existence; and from that time hence I have not held any office, nor do I care to. I only wish I could do a little more for the welfare of my fellow-beings before I depart for another world, as I am now nearly seventy years old, and will soon pass away. I wish my readers to remember that the above history of my existence is only a short outline. If time and means permitted, many more interesting things might be related.

CHAPTER IX.

Some of the Legends of the Ottawa and Chippewa Indians Respecting the Great Flood of the World—A Person Swallowed Up Alive Like a Prophet Jonah.

Before proceeding with the history of the Ottawas and Chippewas some of their most important and peculiar legends will be given. They have a tradition of a great flood, as is recorded it the Bible History, and many other tribes of Indians who speak dialect of the Ottawa and Chippewa languages have the same story. The legends say it was caused, not by a rain, but by the great Ne-naw-bo-zhoo, who was the most remarkable, wonderful, and supernatural being that ever trod upon the earth. He could transfigure himself into the shape of all animals and live with them for a great length of time. He has done much mischief and also many benefits to the inhabitants of the earth whom he called "his nephews;" and he shaped almost everything, teaching his nephews what materials they should take for their future utensils. This mischievous Ne-naw-bo-zhoo spoiled the sugar trees by diluting their sap with water. The legends say, that once upon a time the sugar trees did produce sap at certain season of the year which was almost like a pure syrup; but when this mischievous Ne-naw-bo-zhoo had tasted it, he said to himself, "Ah, that is too cheap. It will not do. My nephews will obtain this sugar too easily in the future time and the sugar will be worthless." And therefore he diluted the sap until he could not taste any sweetness therein. Then he said, "Now my nephews will have to labor hard to make the sugar out of this sap, and the sugar will be much more valuable to them in the future time." In former times the heart of every tree contained fat from which all inhabitants of the earth obtained delicious oil to eat; but this mischievous Ne-naw-bo-zhoo, in his supernatural way, pushed his staff into the heart of every tree; and this is the reason why the heart of every tree has a different color.

There was no great ark in which to float during the great flood, but when Ne-naw-bo-zhoo could not find any more dry land to run to when he was pursued with mountains of water, he said, "let there be a great canoe." So there was a great canoe which he entered with his animals and floated.

As to the origin of Ne-naw-bo-zhee, the legend says, that once upon a time there lived a maiden with her grandmother, who was a very dutiful and obedient child, observing every precept which was taught her by her grandmother, and she spent much time fasting; during which time she had wonderful dreams which she related to her grandmother every morning during her fast days. She very often had a vision of holding conversation with some deities and finally she was assured in a vision, that her children would be terrible and would redeem all the inhabitants of the earth from their various calamities; and accordingly, she bore two sons. The first born was like any other human child, but the last one was a monster which caused the death of its mother, and, although shaped like a human being, as soon as born ran off in the wilderness and was never again seen by any person; but the first child was nourished and reared by the grandmother. When this child grew to be playful and talkative by the side of its grandmother, he was so strange that very often she would say to him, "Your actions are like a Ne-naw-bo-zhoo." Then the child would reply, "I am the great Ne-naw-bo-zhoo on this earth." The meaning of this word in the Algonquin language is "a clown" and therefore he meant that he was the great "clown" of the world.

When Ne-naw-bo-zhoo became a man he was a great prophet for his nephews and an expert hunter. His hunting dog was a great black wolf. When he learned from his grandmother, that his mother was dead and that his brother was a monster with a body like flint stone which caused her death, Ne-naw-bo-zhoo was in a great rage after hearing the story and he determined to seek for this evil being and slay him. Then he immediately prepared for a long journey, and trimmed his ponderous war club nicely and prepared to be in a great battle. So off he went with his great black wolf on the war path. As he passed through the forest, for a trial of his strength and the strength of his war club, he simply made motions with it toward one of the tallest pines of the forest and the gigantic tree came down all into slivers. "Ah," said Ne-naw-bo-zhoo, "who could stand against my strength and the strength of my war club." After many days journey going into every nook and loop hole of the earth, he succeeded at last in having a glimpse of the object of his search. Ne-naw-bo-zhoo ran to overtake him, and chased him all over the world; and every now and then he would be close enough to reach him with his war-club and to strike at him, but he would only break a piece of the monster's stony body, which was like a mountain of hard flint-stone. So the legend says that whenever we find a pile of hard flints lying on the face of the earth, there is where Ne-naw-bo.zhoo overtook his brother monster and struck him with his tremendous war-club. At last he vanquished him on the east shore of Grand Traverse Bay, Michigan, near the place now called Antrim City, but formerly by the Ottawa and Chippewa Indians, it was called "Pe-wa-na-go-ing," meaning "Flinty Point," so called because there were great rocks of flint lying near the edge of the lake shore. And so the Ottawas and Chippewas say it is there where the old carcass of the monster is now lying—the brother of the great Ne-naw-bo-zhoo. After that he traveled over almost every part of this continent sometimes in the shape of an animal and then again in human shape. There is an impression of human foot tracks on a very smooth rock some where along the Ottawa river in Canada, and also a round hole about as large and deep as a common brass kettle on this flat rock near where the track is and every Ottawa and Chippewa calls these "Ne-naw-bo-zhoo's track" and "Ne-naw-bo-zhoo's kettle where he dropped it when chasing his brother," and then they would drop a piece of tobacco in the kettle as a sacrifice, at the same time praying for luck and a prosperous journey to Montreal and back again to Michigan, their native home, when passing this place.

Now the cause of the great flood was this: The god of the deep was exceedingly jealous about Ne-naw-bo-zhoo's hunting dog (the great black wolf) and therefore, he killed it and made a feast with it and invited many guests, which were represented as sea-serpents, water-tigers, and every kind of monster of the deep, and they had a great feast. When Ne-naw-bo-zoo found out what had become of his hunting dog, he was furiously enraged, and determined to kill this god of the deep.

There was a certain place where he was accustomed to come on the shore with his hosts, particularly on very fine days, to sun themselves and enjoy the pleasure of being on a dry land. Ne-naw-bo-zhoo knew this lovely spot very well. So right away he strung up his bow and trimmed his arrows nicely, and went there to watch, transforming himself into a black stump, near where these water gods usually lay down to enjoy themselves. And therefore, one very fine day the sea-serpents and water-tigers were very anxious to come on shore as usual and asked their master to accompany them, but he replied: "I fear the great Ne-naw-bo-zhoo might be lurking about there, and he will kill me because I have killed and eaten up his black wolf." But he at last told them to go on shore and examine the place and report if it was all clear; but they found nothing unusual about the place except the old black stump, which they never before observed to be there. Therefore, they went back to their master and reported that nothing was there to be afraid of except the old black stump which they never noticed before. "Go again," said their master "and closely examine the stump; peradventure, it was he transfigured into the shape of the stump." So again they came ashore and one of the water-tigers climbed upon it, inserting his long, sharp claws as he went up, but he saw nothing strange. So, also the sea-serpent went up to it and coiled himself around the stump so tight that Ne-naw-bo-zhoo nearly screamed with pain. At last the serpent uncoiled himself and they went back to their master and reported to him that it was nothing but an old stump. So the god of the sea concluded to come ashore with all his hosts, slowly and cautiously looking in every direction as he was still afraid that Ne-naw-bo-zhoo might be lurking around there and watching. Soon they were dozing upon the hot sand of the beach, then Ne-naw-bo-zhoo unmasked himself and fixed one of his best arrows into his bow and shot the god of the deep right through the heart. Then all the host started to pursue the slayer of their master. Ne-naw-bo-zhoo fled for his life; but he was pursued by the host with mountains of water. He ran all over the earth, still pursued with the mountains of water. So when he could not find any more dry land to run to, he commanded a great canoe to be formed in which he and the animals who were fleeing before the water, were saved. After they floated, Ne-naw-bo-zhoo wondered very much how deep was the water. Therefore, he ordered one of the beavers to go down to the bottom of the deep and bring up some earth if he could, as evidence that he did go to the bottom. So the beaver obeyed, and he went down, but the water was so deep the beaver died before he reached the bottom, and therefore, he came up floating as a dead beaver. Ne-naw-bo-zhoo drew him up into his canoe and resuscitated the beaver by blowing into his nostrils.

So he waited a little while longer, and afterwards he ordered the muskrat to go down; but the muskrat did not like the idea, for he had seen the beaver coming up lifeless. So he had to flatter him a little in order to induce him to go down, by telling him, "Now, muskrat, I know that thou art one of the best divers of all the animal creation; will you please go down and ascertain the depth of the water, and bring up some earth in your little paws, if you can, with which I shall try to make another world?

Now go my little brother,"—the legend says that he called all the animal creation his little brothers,—"for we cannot always live on the waters." At last the muskrat obeyed. He went down, and descended clear to the bottom of the water, and grabbed the earth and returned. But the water was yet so deep that before he reached the surface of the water, he expired.

As Ne-naw-bo-zhoo drew him up into his great canoe to resuscitate him, he observed the muskrat still grasping something in his little paws, and behold, it was a piece of earth. Then Ne-naw-bo-zhoo knew that the muskrat went clear to the bottom of the deep. He took this piece of earth and fixed it into a small parcel; which he fastened to the neck of the raven which was witn him. Now, with this parcel, Ne-naw-bo-zhoo told the raven to fly to and fro all over the face of the waters; then the waters began to recede very fast, and soon the earth came back to its natural shape, just as it was before.

Again this same Ne-naw-bo-zhoo was once swallowed by a fish, and after being carried about in the midst of the deep, he came out again and lived as well as ever, like the Prophet Jonah. This Ottawa and Chippewa legend is, that once upon a time there was a great fish that resided in a certain lake, and as the people passed through this lake in their canoes, this great fish was accustomed to come after those crossing the lake and if he overtook them he would swallow them up, canoe and all, like swallowing a little clam in its shell. So Ne-naw-bo-zhoo said to himself, "This great fish will eat up all my nephews. Now I must somehow dispose of him." And he went to the lake in his canoe expressly to look for the fish, singing daring songs as he went along. After he came in the midst of it, there he stopped, but kept on singing the following words: "Mishe-la-me-gwe Pe-le-wi-ko-lishim, Pe-la-wi-ko-lishim"—daring the fish to come and swallow him up. So at last the great fish, Mishi-la-me-gwe, did come and swallow the great Ne-naw-bo-zhoo. But this was just what he wanted. After being swallowed, he was able to dispose of this big fish, for with his weapons he caused the fish such pain that he ran on the shore and died. After which, Ne-naw-bo-zhoo came out like the Prophet Jonah, and he went home and sat down to smoke his pipe, perfectly satisfied that he had saved many people by disposing of this great fish.

These are some of the legends told among the Ottawa and Chippewa Indians, as related in their own language, which are in some things quite similar to the records of the Bible.

CHAPTER X.

Traditions of the Ottawas Regarding Their Early History—Their Wars and Their Confederations With Other Tribes of Indians.

Very many centuries ago, before the discovery of the American continent by the white people, the traditions of the Ottawas say they lived along the banks of one of the largest tributaries of the St. Lawrence, now known as the Ottawa river. The Ottawas spread over the country around the head waters of this stream, subduing all other tribes of Indians which they happened to encounter, except the Chippewas and Stockbridge Indians. They have been always friendly and closely related with these tribes, and consequently no war-club was ever raised by either of these against the other. Their language is of the same root, as they could quite intelligently understand each other. Their manners and customs in every way correspond. Their legends, particularly respecting the flood, and their belief in the Supreme Being, the great creator of all things—Ketchi-mat-ne-do—is very much the same; also their belief in the evil spirit, whose habitation was under the earth. To this deity they offered sacrifices as well as to the other gods or deities. These offerings were called in those days peace-offerings and down-offerings. They never sacrificed flesh of animals to the evil spirit. Their offering to this deity was parched corn pounded, then cooked into hominy; this was sacrificed to the evil spirit, not because they loved him, but to appease his wrath.

Although the Chippewas speak almost the same language as the Ottawas and Stockbridge Indians, yet they seem to belong to another family of Indians, as they are much taller than the Ottawas and Stockbridges, and broader across the shoulders—having a full chest, very erect and striding firmly in their walking. They were much more numerous than the Ottawa Indians. They extended from lower Cañada north-westward up to Manitoba county. There are three kinds of Chippewas, each kind having a different dialect. The Chippewas in Canada, around the Straits of Mackinaw, the islands in Lake Michigan, Sault Ste. Marie, and west of Lake Superior, are much more enlightened and intelligent, and these, we called common Chippewas; but those on the plains further north or northwest of Lake Superior, "the wild Chippewas;" and those on the north side of Lake Superior going toward Hudson Bay, we called "the Backwoodsmen." This latter race lived entirely by hunting and fishing and endured very great hardships sometimes, particularly, when there was scarcity of game. The Chippewas were very brave people on the war path, and their principal foes were Sioux Indians on the plains. These were called in the Ottawa language "Naw-do-wa-see," and in the Chippewa "Au-bwan." The plurals are "Naw-do-wa-see-wog" and "Au-bwan-og." The "Naw-do-wa-see-wog" are deadly enemies of the Ottawas and Chippewas, and they are the most careless of their lives, for they taught their children from infancy not to fear death. But the Ottawas were, however, considered as the most ancient tribe of Indians and were called by the other tride "their big brother." Although they are a smaller race, in stature, then many other tribes, they were known as the most wise and sagacious people. Every tribe belonging to all the Algonquin family of Indians looked up to the Ottawas for good counsel; and they were as brave as the Chippewas and very expert on the warpath.

Every tribe of Indians has a different coat of arms, or symbolical sign by which they are known to one another. The emblem of the Ottawas is a moose; of the Chippewas, a sea gull; of the Backswoodsmen, a rabbit; that of the underground tribe, to which I belong, is a species of hawk; and that of the Seneca tribe of Indians is a crotch of a tree. The Ottawa Indians are very nearly extinct in the state of Michigan as there are only two or three families in the state, whose national emblem is a moose, showing them to be descended from pure Ottawa blood; but those who represent ed themselves as the Ottawas in this state are descendants from various tribes of Indians, even some are Senecas, of the Iroquois family—formerly deadly enemies of the Ottawas. The cause of this mixture is by intermarriage, and by prisoners of war in former times.

The first man who signed the treaty of 1836, one of the Chippewas of the Grand River Indians, whose name was "Mixinene," was a descendant of the Backwoodsmen, whose emblem was a rabbit. Therefore, all the rest of those Chippewas who went to Washington to form a treaty with the Government felt displeased about this matter and tried to ignore the signature of Mixinene, because they thought that the first signature should have been made by a pure Ottawa or a pure Chippewa, because they had the first right to the land of Michigan. But the "Backwoodsmen," they considered, had no claim nor title to this land which they ceded to the Government of the United States. But the Government did not know the difference, however,—all she wanted was the land. So all the Chiefs of the Ottawas and Chippewas signed this said treaty, not with free will, but by compulsion.

The tradition gives no reason why the Ottawas continually moved towards the northwest at this early period; but it is, however, supposed that it was on account of their deadly enemies, the Iroquois of New York, as they were continually at war with the six nations of Indians. Quite often, the Iroquois would attack them, but the tradition says that in almost every battle the Ottawas would come out victorious over the Iroquois. The Ottawas too, in retaliation, would go to the Iroquois country to scalp some of the Iroquois; then have their jubilees over these scalps by feasting and dancing around them. At this stage of their existence they were an exceedingly fierce and warlike people, not only contending with these tribes, but also with many others out west and south, even to the Chocktaw and Cherokee country and to the Flatheads, Sioux Indians and the Underground race of people out west.

As the Ottawas continued moving up on this beautiful stream

of water, they at last came to a large lake, the head waters of the river. The surrounding scenery of the lake was most surprisingly beautiful. They immediately named this lake Ke-tchi-ne-bissing, which name it bears to this day. Here the Ottawas concluded to stop and occupy the surrounding country. Therefore, they pitched their tents and formed a great village. They continued to reside around the lake for untold ages. And here too they had many hard battles with the Iroquois; but the Iroquois were not able to conquer them or drive them from the country. But at last the Ottawas became discontented with the place. They concluded that the place was haunted by some presiding deity who was not favorable to them. They probably obtained this idea through having sometimes great disasters in war with the Iroquois at this place. I will here relate an incident which happened to the Ottawas at about this time, and which was the origin of their belief that the deity of the place was unfavorable to them. It may be considered as purely fictitious, but every Ottawa and Chippewa to this day believes it to have actually occurred.

A woman went down to the beach of lake Ke-tchine-bissing to wash some of her clothing, taking along her infant child, which was tied up on a board, according to the fashion of the Indians. When she reached the beach, she set her child down very near the edge of the water that it might watch its mother while at work. Her wigwam stood not far from the lake, and in a few moments she ran to it for something. On her return to the spot she was terribly surprised not to find her child where she had left it but a few minutes before. She ran frantically through the village, crying and screaming, and saying that some one had stolen her baby. A few days after this, two lovers sat upon the top of the highest hillock which stood back of the village. While they were talking very much love to each other, they heard an infant crying bitterly, in the ground directly under them. Every one who heard the report said at once that it must be the same baby who was mysteriously missing on the beach a few days before. The next day all the magicians were called together and requested to divine this mystery. Some went and put themselves into the state of clairvoyance, which was a very common practice among the Ottawas and Chippewas within my time, and is still practiced to-day where there is no Christianity predominating among the Indians. Other magicians built themselves lodges in which to call their favorite spirits in order to commune with them. This, which we might call Spiritualism, was practiced among the Indians much as among the whites at the present day. The form of these lodges was like a tower in circular form built with long poles set deep in the ground ten or twelve feet high, then covered tight all around with canvass or skins of animals, except the top is left open. Now the magician or the performer comes with the little flat magician's rattle like a tamborine. They always build a fire close to the lodge so that the attendants and spectators could light their pipes, as they generally smoke much during the performance. The magician sits by the fire also, and begins to talk to the people, telling them that he could call up various spirits, even the spirit of those who are yet living in the world, and that they should hear them and ask them any questions they wish. After which he begins to sing a peculiar song which scarcely any-one could understand. Then he either goes into the lodge by crawling under, or sits out side with the rest of the audience, and simply throws something of his wear in the lodge—his blanket or his robe or coat. And immediately the lodge begins to tremble, appearing to be full of wind. Then voices of various kinds are heard from top to bottom, some speaking in unknown tongues, and when the spectators ask any questions they would receive replies sometimes with unknown tongues, but among the spirits there is always a special interpreter to make known what other spirits says.

After the magicians had finished their incantations, one of them, whom they thought greatest of all, went down to the beach to the place where the child had been missing. The water was very deep there along the beach quite close to the shore. He plunged in the lake and was gone under water for a long time. At last he came up and reported that he had discovered a doorway under deep water for a passage which seemed to lead toward the top of the hill. He believed through this passage the child was conveyed to the top of the hill by some evil monster, and all the rest of the magicians agreed with this opinion. Therefore, they returned to their village to hold another council and they concluded to dig down wherever the magicians would direct and try to find the passage. They found the passage after making a very deep hole which to this day is said to be yet visible at Ke-tchine-bissing. While they were digging, two supernatural monsters ran out of the place; and at last at the top of the hill they found a cavern where the dead form of the child was discovered.

CHAPTER XI.

The Ottawas Moving Again Towards the Setting Sun—Coming to Manitoulin, or Ottawa Island—The Names of Their Leaders—The Wenebago Warriors Coming to Ottawa Island in a Hostile Manner, Headed by O-saw-wa-ne me-kee, "The Yellow Thunder"—Death of Kaw-be-naw, one of the Greatest Prophets and Warriors of the Ottawas—Massacre in the Country of Waw-gaw-na-ke-zhe, or Arbor Croche, Emmet County, Michigan.

Soon after the loss of the child, the Ottawas abandoned the country and again moved toward the setting sun until they came to Lake Huron. Here they discovered a great island which is now called Manitoulin, but formerly, the Ottawa Island. Here the Ottawas remained for many more centuries. Here too, was born one of the greatest warriors and prophets that the Ottawas ever had, whose name was Kaw-be-naw. This word is accented on the last syllable,—its definition is—"He would be brought out." There are many curious and interesting adventures related of this great warrior and prophet, a record of which would require a large book. But I will here give one of the last acts of his life. It is related that he became tired of living and killing so many people. He desired to die; but he could not. It is also related that the We-ne-be-go tribe of Indians had also one man who was almost equal in power to Kaw-be-naw whose name was "O-saw-wa-ne-me-kee"—the "Yellow Thunder." Having heard the fame of Kaw-be-naw, he was very anxious to meet him on the war path that he might have an opportunity to contend with him in battle. And consequently he formed a most enormous expedition to the Island with his numerous warriors expressly to meet Kaw-be-naw. But Kaw-be-naw knowing everything that was going on in the Wenebago country, told his people to prepare for a great war, for numerous Wenebagoes were coming to the Island headed with O-so-wa-waw-ne-me-kee in a very hostile manner.

At last O-saw-wa-ne-me-kee landed with his warriors on the Island, and marched towards the largest village of the Ottawas, which was situated in the interior of the Island where there was a lake. So Kaw-be-naw starts with his wife, pretending that he was going after cedar bark, but his real object was to meet the Wenebagoes on their march toward the village. When he saw the Wenebagoes coming, he told his wife to run home quickly and tell nobody what she had seen, and he alone went to meet them. When they saw him he did not try to get away, so they easily captured him. Of course the Wenebagoes knew not that he was the very man they were seeking. They asked him many questions as to the condition of the Ottawas, how many there were in the village, and whether Kaw-be-naw was at home or not. He told them the Ottawas were in good condition to fight, but Kaw-be-naw was not at home just then, but would probably be home by to-morrow or day after, as he was gone only to get cedar bark somewhere. The Wenebegoes made a deep pit in the ground and after tieing Kaw-be-naw they threw him in the pit and covered him with heavy stones and dirt and then marched on.

When they came in view of the village they halted. They concluded that they would not make the attack until morning. Kaw-be-naw, after lying awhile in the pit, magically released himself and went home, and told his people that the Wenebagoes were very close at hand; and by to-morrow there would be a great battle, so every man must be well prepared. The village was in terrible anxiety that night, the women and children were all gathered in one place and the warriors in another, and the village was well guarded. Early in the morning the war cry was heard, and every warrior went forward to meet the Wenebagoes, but Kaw-be-naw remained in his lodge while his warriors were fighting. The old O-so-waw-ne-me-kee was nearly naked and frightfully painted from head to foot, so that he looked more like a demon than a human being. Of course he did not know who might be Kaw-be-naw among the Ottawas, therefore he sang out, saying, "Where is your great Kaw-be-naw? I should like to meet him in this battle." So one of the warriors replied, "Don't you know that you have buried our great Kaw-be-naw in the pit yesterday?" "Thanks to the Great Spirit for delivering the Ottawas into my hands," said old O-so-waw-ne-me-kee triumphantly. Just then, Kaw-be-naw came out of his lodge in full uniform of black bear skins, with his ponderous war club in his hand, and mocked his antagonist by saying, "Thanks to the Great Spirit, here I am; and now meet me all you want." Kaw-be-naw looked so grand and noble, and was such an extraordinary personage that O-so-waw-ne-me-kee did not know what to do with himself, whether to yield or to fight. But remembering his previous threats, he made out to face him. However Kaw-be-naw did not take long to dispose of him; O-so-waw-ne-me-kee was soon slain. When the Wenebagoes saw that their great warriar was no more, they immediately raised a flag of truce, and requested that they might acknowledge themselves as conquered and depart in peace.

During the affray with O-so-waw-ne-me-kee, Kaw-be-naw received a little scratch on his nose which drew a few drops of his blood, and therefore when he saw a flag of truce he disarmed himself and went to the Wenebagoes, saying, "O, you have killed me." The Wenebagoes said, "How and where?" "Don't you see the blood on my nose?" "Pshaw, that is only a scratch," said the Wenebagoes. "Well, that very thing will cause me to die." The Wenebagoes tried to send him away, but he would not leave them. At last they took him prisoner. They tied him with small strong cord which every warrior generally carries in case of capture. As they journeyed towards their home one fine day, they began to council about him, saying, "This man will never die. When we get him into our country, he will make a terrible slaughter among our women and children. We better dispose of him before we reach home." So they concluded to sink him into deep water. Therefore they tied a big stone about his neck and put him overboard. They went on rejoicing and traveled all day in their canoes, thinking that they had disposed of the greatest man in the world and were very much elated at the idea; forgetting how he had once escaped after being buried in a deep pit. When evening came, they encamped for the night. While they were preparing their food, they saw a man coming along on the beach toward them who appeared to them like Kaw-be-naw. The Wenebagoes were in terrible consternation. Soon he came up to them, and behold it was he. Then the Wenebagoes were in great terror. But as he came up to them he spoke very pleasently, saying, "Ho, what a pleasent journey we have had to-day. Well, children, have you any meat? I am getting quite hungry after traveling all day." Of course they had to treat him as well as they could, and Kaw-be naw came into the midst of them. That night the Wenebagoes lay awake all night, and they thought every moment they would be slaughtered by Kaw-be-naw in revenge for trying to drown him. In the morning after breakfast as they were preparing to go Kaw-be-naw spoke to them saying, "Children, if you want to kill me, I will tell you how. You must take all the flesh from off my body by cutting it piece by piece with your knives, and leave no flesh upon my bones; for this is the only way that I can be killed." The Wenebagoes were terribly frightened as they thought that so soon as any one would touch him he would kill every Wenebago. So they held a council to determine what they should do. But the majority were in favor of performing this dreadful act, as Kaw-be-naw ordered, for he desired to die. When they came back, Kaw-be-naw persisted that they should begin, and assured them that he would never resist. At last, one of the bravest Wenebagoes went up to him and cut a piece of his flesh. Kaw-be-naw never stirred but simply smiled and said, "That is the way you must do. What are you afraid of? Come all ye who have sharp knives." Pretty soon they were all around him taking his flesh piece after piece. When it was all done he said, "It is finished; now I shall surely die. But as recompense for my flesh and life a great battle will be made against you by my sncccessor, and as many of your best young men shall fall in this battle as pieces have been cut from my flesh." At the end of this sentence, he fell backwards and died. Thus ended the career of the great Kaw-be-naw, the Ottawa warrior and prophet.

"Shaw-ko-we-sy" was the successor of Kaw-be naw and was almost equal in power to his predecessor. It is related that in the following year, he went to the Wenebago country with his numerous warriors and killed many Wenebagoes, as many as Kaw-be-naw predicted, and returned late in the fall to their Island with many of the Wenebagoes' scalps. While they were having jubilees, festivities, and war dances over these scalps of the Wenebagoes, in the dead of winter, the tribe of Michilimackinawgoes, the remnant race of Indians who resided at the Island now called Mackinac, whose fate has been given in a previous chapter, were destroyed. This is the time, according to the Ottawa traditions, that the Iroquois of New York came upon this race of people and almost entirely annihilated them, and the Ottawas and Chippewas called this Island Michilimackinong in order to perpetuate the name of these unfortunate Indians.

There were also a small tribe of Indians, beside the Chippewas, that resided on the north side of the strait whose principal village was situated at the place now called St. Ignace, but the Ottawas and Chippewas call this place to this day "Naw-do-we-que-yah-mi-shen-ing," which is a compound name from "Naw-do-we," the name of the tribe who resided there, and "Na-yah-me-shen, point of land in water. And afterwards part of the Ottawas came over from their Island and resided with them, during the days of old Saw-ge-maw, who was one of the great warriors and leaders of the Ottawas. But afterwards Saw-ge-maw quarreled with them and broke up the confederacy and drove them off. Here, too, at about this time, part of the Ottawas left the country in anger because they were cheated out of one of the great feasts they were having on some particular occasion. These went far west and joined the Sho-sho-nee tribe of Indians, whose country lies on the side of the Rocky Mountains, and consequently the Ottawa language is quite extensively spoken among that tribe of Indians to this day.

The south side of the straits, which now constitutes Emmet, Cheboygan and Charlevoix counties, our tradition says, was exceedingly thickly populated by another race of Indians, whom the Ottawas called Mush-co-desh, which means, "the Prairie tribe." They were so called on account of being great cultivators of the soil, and making the woodland into prairie as they abandoned their old worn out gardens which formed grassy plains. It is related, this tribe was quite peaceable, and were never known to go on a warpath. The Ottawas of Manitoulin had joined hands with them as their confederates. They called each other "brothers." But on one of the western war trips of the great Saw-ge-maw, who existed about the time America was first discovered by white men, he met with great disaster, as many of his warriors were killed; so on returning homeward with his remaining survivors, they crossed Little Traverse Bay in a canoe and approached the shores of Arbor Croche at the place now called Seven Mile Point, where there was a large village of Mush-co-desh. Saw-ge-maw said to his few warriors, "Let us take our sad news to our relations the Mush-co-desh." So as they approached the shore they began to make an unearthly wailing noise, according to the custom of the Ottawas, which was called the death song of the warriors. When the Mush-co-dish heard them they said to one another, "Hark, the Ottawas are crying. They have been marauding among some tribes in the west; but this time they have been worsted—good enough for them. See, they are coming ashore. Let us not permit them to land." So instead of preparing to join in their mourning, as would have been proper, they rashly determined to express their disapproval of the marauding expeditions and their contempt for those who engaged in them. Before Saw-ge-maw had fairly touched the beach, parties of Mush-co-desh ran down to the shore with balls of ashes wrapped up in forest leaves and with these they pelted Saw-ge-maw and his party as they came ashore. This treatment dreadfully provoked Saw-ge-maw, and the insult was such as could only be wiped out with blood. He told his warriors to pull homeward as quickly as possible. "We will come back here in a few days; we will not have to go so far again to look for our enemies." Arriving at Manitoulin Island, he immediately prepared for a great war. After they were completely equipped, they came back to the southern peninsula of Michigan, stealthily and carefully landing at the most uninhabited part of the shore. They then marched to one of the largest villages of Mush-co-desh, which was situated between Cross Village and Little Traverse, in a beautiful valley in the northern part of the township now called Friendship. Arriving late in the afternoon within view of the village, the Ottawas hid in ambush. One of the old women of the Mush-co-dosh was going through the bushes looking for young basswood bark from which to manufacture twine or cord. She came right where the Ottawas were lying in ambush. She was terribly surprised, but the Ottawas persuaded her not to reveal their presence by telling her they would give her a young man as her husband, pointing to one of the best looking young warriors there. They told her, early in the morning they were going to fall upon the village and kill every one of the Mush-co-desh, but when she heard the war-whoop she must run to them and she should not be killed but be protected. The foolish woman believed and kept the secret. Early in the morning the war cry was heard, and she ran to the Ottawas to be protected, but she was the first one to be slain. It was indeed a terrible calamity for the Mush-co-desh. At the begining of the noise of massacre, the chief of the Mush-co-desh ran forward and screamed loud as he could, saying, "O! My father, Saw-ge-maw, what is the cause of your coming upon us so suddenly with death, as we have never wronged your race?" "Have you already forgotten" said Saw-ge-maw triumphantly, "that you have greatly insulted me on your borders? You have pelted me with ashes when I was lamenting over the loss of my braves." When the Mush-co-desh saw they could not prevail on Saw-ge-maw, nor could withstand an adversary so formidable and such well prepared warriors, they endeavored to flee, but they were overtaken and slaughtered. Only the swift-footed young men escaped, taking the sad message to other villages of Mush-co-desh, and as fast as the news reached them they fled with their women and children toward the south along the shore of Lake Michigan, and continued to fly, although they were not pursued by the Ottawas, till they reached the St. Joseph River, and there they stopped, and formed a union village, and began to cultivate the soil again.

The tradition says this was the greatest slaughter or massacre the Ottawas ever committed. The inhabitants of this village were probably from forty to fifty thousand. There were many other villages of Mush-co-desh of minor importance everywhere scattered through the northern part of the southern peninsula of Michigan. Where this doomed village was situated is yet to this day distinctly visible, as there are some little openings and trails not overgrown by the forest.

Soon after this the Ottawas abandoned their island and came over and took possession of the country of the Mush-co-desh. Most of them settled at the place now called Magulpin's Point, where the present lighthouse is situated, near old Mackinac. At the time the French settled in Montreal, Au-tche-a, one of the Ottawa prophets, told his people there were some strange persons living in this continent, who were far superior to any other inhabitants upon the earth. So Au-tche-a determined to search for these wonderful people and he persuaded five of his neighbors to accompany him in his undertaking. They started out, but they went a very roundabout way, and it was a long time before they came to the Ottawa river; then floating down they came out on the St. Lawrence. They were gone for more than a year. When they came where the white men were, they first saw a vessel or ship anchored in the middle of the St. Lawrence, which they thought was a monster waiting to devour them as they came along. But as they neared it they saw some, people on the back of the monster. So Autchea and his party were taken on board, add his little frail canoe was hoisted into the ship. They found some Stockbridge Indians there also, who spoke a dialect of their language. After exchanging all they had, and learning how to handle firearms, they started back again to the straits of Mackinac. The tradition says, they arrived at their village on an exceedingly calm day, and the water was in perfect stillness in the straits. The Indians saw the canoe coming towards the shore of the village, when suddenly a puff of smoke was seen and a terrific clash of sound followed immediately. All the inhabitants were panic stricken, and thought it was something supernatural approaching the shore. But again and again they witnessed the same thing, as it came nearer and nearer. At last they recognized the great prophet Au-tche-a and his party coming back from his long trip, having found his "Manitou" that he was looking after. The reader may imagine how it was, when Au-tche-a landed and exhibited his strange articles—his gun with its belongings, his axes, his knives, his new mode of making fire, his cooking utensils, his clothing and his blankets. It was no small curiosity to the aborigines.

The Ottawas gradually extended their settlements towards the south, along the shore of Lake Michigan. The word Michigan is an Indian name, which we pronounce Mi-chi-gum, and simply means "monstrous lake." My own ancestors, the Undergrounds, settled at Detroit, and they considered this was the extent of their possessions. But the greatest part of the Ottawas settled at Arbor Croche, which I have already related as being a continuous village some fifteen miles long. But in the forest of this country were not many deer, and consequently when the winter approached most of the Indians went south to hunt, returning again in the spring loaded with dry meat.

The Mush-co-desh were not long in safety in the southern part of the state. Intercourse had been opened between the French and the Ottawas and Chippewas on the straits of Mackinac and being supplied with fire arme and axes by the French people, it occurred to the Ottawas that these impliments would be effective in battle. Anxious to put them to the test, they resolved to try them on their old enemies, the Mush-co-desh, who had not yet seen the white man and were unacquainted with firearms. Accordingly an expedition was fitted out. As the Ottawas approached the village of their enemies, each carrying a gun, the Mush-co-desh thought they were nothing but clubs, so came out with their bows and arrows, anticipating an easy victory. But they soon found out that they were mistaken. As the Ottawas came up they suddenly halted, not near enough to be reached by any arrows of Mush-co-desh, but the Ottawas began to fire away with their guns. Poor Mush-co-desh; they suffered more than ever in this second crushing defeat. The Ottawas left only one family of Mush-co-desh at this time and these went west somewhere to find a new home. My father and my uncles in their younger days while they were making a tour out west, happened to come across the descendants of this nearly anihilated tribe of Indians. They had grown to nine lodges only at that time, and they visited them in a friendly manner. The old warriors wept as they were conversins with them on their terrible calamities and misfortunes and their being once powerful allies and closely related; for these few still remembered the past, and what had become of their ancestors.

After the Ottawas took complete possession of the southern peninsula of Michigan, they fought some more tribes of Indians, subdued them, and compelled them to form confederation with them as their allies. Such as Po-to-wa-to-mies, Mano-me-mis, O-daw-gaw-mies, Urons and Assawgies, who formerly occupied Saw-ge-naw-bay. Therefore the word Saginaw is derived from the name Os-saw-gees, who formerly lived there. They have been always closely united with the Chippewas and very often they went together on the warpath, except at one time they nearly fought on account of a murder, as has been herein related. Also the Shaw-wa-nee tribe of Indians were always closely related to them.

But the Ottawa nation of Indians are always considered as the oldest and most expert on the warpath and wise councilors; and consequently every tribe of Indians far and near, even as far as the Manitoba country, out north, deposited their pipe of peace with the head chief of the Ottawa nation as a pledge of continual peace and friendship. Every pipe of peace contained a short friendly address which must be committed to memory by every speaker in the council of the Ottawas. If there was ever any outbreak among these tribes who deposited their pipe of peace with the head chief of the Ottawa nation, a general council would be called by the chiefs of the Ottawas, and the pipe of peace belonging to the tribe who caused the trouble would be lighted up, and the short address contained in the pipe would be repeated in the council by one of the speakers. When the cause of the outbreak or trouble was ascertained, then reconciliation must be had, and friendly relation must be restored, in which case they almost invariably succeeded in making some kind of reasonable settlement. This was the custom of all these people; and this is what formerly constituted the great Algonquin family of Indians.

There are many theories as to the origin of the Indian race in America, but nothing but speculation can be given on this subject. But we believe there must have been people living in this country before those tribes who were driven out by the Ottawas and Chippewas, who were much more advanced in art and in civilization, for many evidences of their work have been discoved. About two hundred and fifty years ago, We-me-gen-de-bay, one of our noted chiefs, discovered while hunting in the wilderness a great copper kettle, which was partly in the ground. The roots of trees had grown around it and over it, and when it was taken up it appeared as if it had never been used, but seemed to be just as it came from the maker, as there was yet a round bright spot in the center of the bottom of it. This kettle was large enough to cook a whole deer or bear in it. For a long time the Indians kept it as a sacred relic. They did not keep it near their premises, but securely hidden in a place most unfrequented by any human being. They did not use it for anything except for great feastt. Their idea with regard to this kettle was that it was made by some deity who presided over the country where it was found, and that the copper mine must be very close by where the kettle was discovered. Gne peculiarity of its manufacture was that it had no iron rim around it, nor bail for hanging while in use, as kettles are usually made, but the edge of the upper part was much thicker than the rest and was turned out square about three-fourths of an inch, as if made to rest on some support while in use. When the Indians came to be civilized in Grand Traverse country, they began to use this "Mani-tou-au-kick," as they called it, in common to boil tne sugar sap in it, instead of cooking bear for the feast. And while I was yet in the government blacksmith shop at the Old Mission in Grand Traverse, they brought this magical kettle to our shop with an order to put an iron rim and bail on it so that it could be hanged in boiling sugar, and I did the work of fixing the kettle according to the order.

From this evidence of working in metals and from the many other relics of former occupants, it is evident that this country has been inhabited for many ages, but whether by descendants of the Jews or of other Eastern races there is no way for us to determine.

CHAPTER XII.

The Present Condition of the Indians of this State.

Some histories have been written by white men of events since the Ottawa and Chippewa Indians came in contact with white people in this part of the country, but here is given the history of this race of Indians before that time. This account of the Ottawa and Chippewa Indians is of as much interest to every inquirer into the histories of nations, as that of any other people; and all philanthropic people, and those who are endeavoring to enlighten and Christianize the Indians, will feel deeply interested in becoming acquainted with the past history as well as the present condition of these once numerous and warlike people.

There are now but comparatively few living in the State of Michigan, trying to become civilized and to imitate their white neighbors in agricultural industries and other civilized labors. The greater part of them are being Christianized and are members of various Christian churches of the country, erecting houses of worship with their own hands in which to worship the true God in spirit and in truth. A few of them are becoming native preachers and expounders of the Gospel.

A treaty was concluded in the city of Washington in the year 1836, to which my people—the Ottawas and Chippewas—were unwilling parties, but they were compelled to sign blindly and ignorant of the true spirit of the treaty and the true import of some of its conditions. They thought when signing the treaty that they were securing reservations of lands in different localities as permanent homes for themselves and their children in the future; but before six months had elapsed from the time of signing this treaty, or soon after it had been put in pamphlet form so that all persons could read it and know its terms, they were told by their white neighbors that their reservations of land would expire in five years, instead of being perpetual, as they believed. At the end of this time, they would be compelled to leave their homes, and if they should refuse they would be driven at the point of the bayonet into a strange land, where, as is almost always the case, more than one-half would die before they could be acclimated. At this most startling intelligence more than half of my people fled into Canada; fled to the protection of the British government; fled, many of them, even before receiving a single copper of the promised annuities; fled to a latitude like that in which they had been accustomed to live. The balance of them determined to remain and await whatever the consequences might be, and receive the annuities which they were promised for twenty years. But fortunately their expulsion from the State was suddenly stayed, in the years 1850 and '51. By the kindness of the people of the State of Michigan, they were adopted as citizens and made equal in rights with their white neighbors. Their voice was to be recognized in the ballot box in every election; and I thought, this is what ought to be, for the same God who created the white man created the red man of the forest, and therefore they are equally entitled to the benefits of civilization, education and Christianity.

At that time I was one of the principal ones who advocated this cause, for I had already received a partial education, and in my understanding of this matter, I thought that was the only salvation of my people from being sent off to the west of the Mississippi. In laboring for this object, I suffered very great hardship and many struggles, but was at last successful.

But in order that my people can enjoy every privilege of civilization, they must be thoroughly educated; they must become acquainted with the arts and sciences, as well as the white man. Soon as the Indian youths receive an education, they should be allowed to have some employment among the whites, in order to encourage them in the pursuits of civilization and to exercise their ability according to the means and extent of their education, instead of being a class of persons continually persecuted and cheated and robbed of their little possessions. They should have been educated amongst the civilized communities in order to learn the manners and customs of the white people. If this method could have been pursued in the first instance, the aborigines of this country would have secured all the advantages of civilization, education and Christianity. This was my plan and my proposition at the council of Detroit, in the treaty of 1855, as there was quite a large sum of money set apart and appropriated by the Government for the education of Indian youth of the Ottawa and Chippewa Indians of Michigan, and I made the proposition at this council that the sum for that purpose be retained in the hands of the Government solely to pay for the education of those Indian youths who should be educated in a civilized community, instead of committing this sum of money to the hands of the preachers and teachers in the missions among the Ottawas and Chippewas. If my plan could have been adopted, even as late as thirty-two years ago, we should have had, by this time, many well-educated Indians in this State, and probably some good farmers, and perhaps some noted professors of sciences would have been developed, and consequently happiness, blessings and prosperity would have been everywhere among the aborigines of the State of Michigan.

CHAPTER XIII.

The Lamentation of the Overflowing Heart of the Red Man of the Forest.

Hark! What is that I hear,
So mournfully ringing in my ear,
Like a death song of warriors,
For those who fell by their brave sires?
Is this the wail now sounding
For my unhappy future?

O my destiny, my destiny! How sinks my heart, as I behold my inheritance all in ruins and desolation. Yes, desolation; the land the Great Spirit has given us in which to live, to roam, to hunt, and build our council fires, is no more to behold. Where once so many brave Algonquins and the daughters of the forest danced with joy, danced with gratitude to the Great Spirit for their homes, they are no more seen. Our forests are gone, and our game is destroyed. Hills, groves and dales once clad in rich mantle of verdure are stripped. Where is this promised land which the Great Spirit had given to his red children as the perpetual inheritance of their posterity from generation to generation? Ah, the pale-faces who have left their fathers' land, far beyond the ocean, have now come and dispossessed us of our heritage with cruel deceit and force of arms. Still are they rolling on, and rolling on, like a mighty spray from the deep ocean, overwhelming the habitations of nature's children. Is it for the deeds of Pocahontas, of Massasoit, of Logan, and hosts of others who have met and welcomed the white men in their frail cabin doors when they were few in numbers, cold and hungry? Is it for this that we have been plundered, and expelled at the point of the bayonet from the hallowed graves of our brothers and sires? O, my father, thou hast taught me from my infancy to love this land of my birth; thou hast even taught me to say that "it is the gift of the Great Spirit," when yet my beloved mother clasped me close to her peaceful breast while she sang of the warlike deeds of the great Algonquins. O, my father, our happiest days are o'er, and never again shall we enjoy our forest home. The eagle's eye could not even discover where once stood thy wigwam and thy peacefnl council fire. Ah, once it was the happy land, and all the charms were there which made every Indian heart swell with thanks to the Great Spirit for their happy homes. Melodious music was heard in every grove, sung by the wild birds of the forest, who mingled their notes sweetly with the wild chant of my beloved sisters at eve. They sang the song of lullaby to the pawpose of the red man whilst swinging in the cradle from the shady trees, wafted gracefully to and fro by the restless wind. The beautiful old basswood tree bending so gracefully stood there, and the brown thrush sang with her musical voice. That tree was planted there by the Great Spirit for me to sport under, when I could scarcely bend my little bow. Ah, I watched that tree from childhood to manhood, and it was the dearest spot to me in this wide world. Many happy youthful days have I spent under this beautiful shady tree. But alas, alas, the white man's ax has been there! The tree that my good spirit had planted for me, where once the pretty brown thrush daily sat with her musical voice, is cut down by the ruthless hands of the white man. 'Tis gone; gone forever and mingled with the dust. Oh, my happy little bird, thy warbling songs have ceased, and thy voice shall never again be heard on that beautiful shady tree. My charming bird, how oft thou hast aroused me from my slumber at early morn with thy melodious song. Ah, could we but once more return to our forest glade and tread as formerly upon the soil with proud and happy heart! On the hills with bended bow, while nature's flowers bloomed all around the habitation of nature's child, our brothers once abounded, free as the mountain air, and their glad shouts resounded from vale to vale, as they chased o'er the hills the mountain roe and followed in the otter's track. Oh return, return! Ah, never again shall this time return. It is gone, and gone forever like a spirit passed. The red man will never live happy nor die happy here any more. 'Tis passed, 'tis done. The bow and quiver with which I have shot many thousands of game is useless to me now, for the game is destroyed. When the white man took every foot of my inheritance, he thought to him I should be the slave. Ah, never, never! I would sooner plunge the dagger into my beating heart, and follow the footsteps of my forefathers, than be slave to the white man.

MACK-E-TE-BE-NESSY.

CHAPTER XIV.

The Twenty-one Precepts or Moral Commandments of the Ottawa and Chippewa Indians, by Which They Were Governed in Their Primitive State, Before They Came in Contact With White Races in Their Country—The Ten Commandments, The Creed, and The Lord's Prayer in the Ottawa Language as Translated by the Author.

1st. Thou shalt fear the Great Creator, who is the over ruler of all things.

2d. Thou shalt not commit any crime, either by night or by by day, or in a covered place: for the Great Spirit is looking upon thee always, and thy crime shall be manifested in time, thou knowest not when, which shall be to thy disgrace and shame.

3d. Look up to the skies often, by day and by night, and see the sun, moon and stars which shineth in the firmament, and think that the Great Spirit is looking upon thee continually.

4th. Thou shalt not mimic or mock the thunders of the cloud, for they were specially created to water the earth and to keep down all the evil monsters that are under the earth, which would eat up and devour the inhabitants of the earth if they were set at liberty.

5th. Thou shalt not mimic or mock any mountains or rivers, or any prominent formation of the earth, for it is the habitation of some deity or spirit of the earth, and thy life shall be continually in hazard if thou shouldst provoke the anger of these deities.

6th. Honor thy father and thy mother, that thy days may be long upon the land.

7th. Honor the gray-head persons, that thy head may also be like unto theirs.

8th. Thou shalt not mimic or ridicule the cripple, the lame, or deformed, for thou shall be crippled thyself like unto them if thou shouldst provoke the Great Spirit.

9th. Hold thy peace, and answer not back, when thy father or thy mother or any aged person should chastise thee for thy wrong.

10th. Thou shalt never tell a falsehood to thy parents, nor to thy neighbors, but be always upright in thy words and in thy dealings with thy neighbors.

11th. Thou shalt not steal anything from thy neighbor, nor covet anything that is his.

12th. Thou shalt always feed the hungry and the stranger.

13th. Thou shalt keep away from licentiousness and all other lascivious habits, nor utter indecent language before thy neighbor and the stranger.

14th. Thou shalt not commit murder while thou art in dispute with thy neighbor, unless it be whilst on the warpath.

15th. Thou shalt chastise thy children with the rod whilst they are in thy power.

16th. Thou shalt disfigure thy face with charcoals, and fast at least ten days or more of each year, whilst thou are yet young, or before thou reachest twenty, that thou mayest dream of thy future destiny.

17th. Thou shalt immerse thy body into the lake or river at least ten days in succession in the early part of the spring of the year, that thy body may be strong and swift of foot to chase the game and on the warpath.

18th. At certain times with thy wife or thy daughters, thou shalt clean out thy fireplaces and make thyself a new fire with thy fire-sticks for the sake of thyself and for the sake of thy childrens' health.

19th. Thou shalt not eat with thy wife and daughters at such time, of food cooked on a new fire, but they shall be provided with a separate kettle and cook their victuals therein with an old fire and out of their wigwam, until the time is passed, then thou shalt eat with them.*

20th. Thou shalt not be lazy, nor be a vagabond of the earth, to be hated by all men.

21st. Thou shalt be brave, and not fear any death.

If thou shouldst observe all these commandments, when thou diest thy spirit shall go straightway to that happy land where all the good spirits are, and shall there continually dance with the beating of the drum of Tchi-baw-yaw-booz, the head spirit in the spirit land. But if thou shouldst not observe them, thy spirit shall be a vagabond of the earth always, and go hungry, and will never be able to find this road, "Tchi-bay-kon," in which all the good spirits travel.

THE TEN COMMANDMENTS.

1st. Pay-zhe-go ke-zhe-maw-nito me-so-de kay-go kaw-ge-zhe-tod; ke-gaw-pay-zhe-go gwaw-nawdji-aw ane-go-ko-day-a-you ke-gaw-pay-zhe-go saw-ge-aw.

2d. Kaw-we aw-nesh ke-zhe-maw-nito ke-gaw-wo-we nossi.

3d. Au-nwe-be-we-ne-ge-zhe-got ke-gaw-kwaw-nawdji-ton.

4th. Kouss kanie ke-gaw-she ke-gaw-me-naw-tene-mawg ke-nwezh tchi-we-pe-maw-deze-yan aw-zhon-daw aw-king.

5th. Ke-go au-we-yaw me-saw-wa-ne-maw-gay.

6th. Ke-go nau-nawe e-nau-de-se-kay.

7th. Ke-go ke-mou-de-kay.

8th. Ke-go kawie ke-no-wish-ke-kay tche-baw-taw-maw-de-baw au-we-ya.

9th. Ke-go mes-sau-we-naw-mau-we-ye-gay ke-dji-pe-maw-de-si o-we-de-gay-maw-gaw-non.

10th. Ke-go kauie au-we-yaw mes-saw-wendau mau-we-ye-gay ke-go andaw-nedji.

THE CREED.

Men da-bwe-taw-waw Pa-zhe-go maw-nito we-osse-mind, me-zo-day ke-go nay-taw-we-tod, kaw-ge-zhe-tod wau-kwee aw-ke kauie.

* See Dr. Bondinot's work, "The Star in the West," pp. 216 and 225.

Men day-bwe-taw-we-mon knice ogwisson paw-ye-zhe-go-nedjin Jesus Krist te-bay-ne-me-nong. We-ne-zhe-she-nedjin maw-niton o-ge-aw-neshe-naw-bay-we-egoun, Mari-yon kaw-gaw-ge we-nedjin oge-ne-ge-egoun. Ke-go-daw-ge-to me-gwaw o-ge-maw-wit Ponce Pila-tawn, ke-baw-daw-kaw-ko-wou tche-baw-yaw-te-gong, ke-ne-bon ke-naw-gwo-wau kauie au-naw-maw-kaw-mig ke-e-zhaw, waw-ne-so-ke-zhe-te-nig Ke-au-be-tchi-baw. Waw-kwing ke-e-zhaw, naw-maw-daw-be o-day-baw-ne-we-kaw-ning ke-zle-maw-niton way-osse me-medjin me-zo-day ke-go nay tau-we-to-nedjin me-dawst waw-de-be ke-be-ondji-bawd, tche-be-te-baw-ko-nod pay-maw-de-ze-nedjin, nay-bo-nedjin kauie. Men day-bwe-taw-waw Way-ne-zhe-shed maw-nito, men day-bwe-tawn kitche-two kaw-to-lic au-naw-me-a-we-gaw-mig, kay-tchi-two-wendaw-go-ze-djig o-we-do-ko-daw-de-we-ne-wau paw-taw-do-wene kawss-au-maw-gay-win aw-bedji-baw-win ezhe-owe-yossing kaw-go-ne pe-maw-de-se-win. Aw-pe-inge.

THE LORD'S PRAYER.

Nossinaw wau-kwing e-be-you au-pe-gwish ke-tchi-twaw-wend-oming ke-daw-no-zo-win, au-pe-gish pe-daw-gwe-she-no-maw-gok ke-do-gimaw-o-win, ena-daw-mon au-pe-gish ezhe-wa-bawk, ti-bish-wau-kwing mego kauie au-king. Me-zhe-she-nong nongo au-gi-zhe-gawk nin baw-kwe-zhe-gaw-ne-me-naw menik e-you-yong en-daw-so ke-zhe-gok. Po-ne-ge-tay-taw-we-shi-nong kauie kaw-nish ki-e-nange te-bish-kon ezhe-pone-ge-day-taw-wou-ge-dwaw kaw-neshke-e-yo-mendjig, ke-go kauie ezhe-we-zhe-she-kong-gay kaw-gwe ti-bandji-gay-we-ning, au-tchi-tchaw-yo-ing dansh etaw eni-naw-maw-we-she-nong maw-tchaw-go-e-wish. Ken maw-ke-daw-yon o-ge-maw-owen, mawsh-kaw-we-se-win kauie pe-she-gain-daw-go-se-win, kaw-ge-gay-kow-mig au-pe-nay dash kau-e-go kaw-ge-nig. Amen.

GRAMMAR

—OF THE—

OTTAWA AND CHIPPEWA LANGUAGE.

NOUNS.

Common nouns in the Ottawa and Chippewa language are divided into two classes, animate and inanimate. Animate nouns are those which signify living objects or objects supposed to have life, as persons, animals and plants. Inanimate nouns signify objects without life.

A third form of nouns is derived from these two classes, called diminutive nouns. These are formed by the termination "ens" or "ns" placed upon other nouns.

The plural of animate nouns is usually formed by adding the syllable "wog" to the singular; if the word ends in a vowel, only the letter "g" is added; and sometimes the syllables "yog," "ag," or "og."

All words are pronounced with accent on the last syllable.

Sing.	Pl.	Eng.
Pe-nay,	Pe-nay-wog,	Partridge.
Aw-dje-djawk,	Aw-dje-djaw-wog,	Crane.
Waw-mawsh-kay-she,	Waw-mawsh-kay-she-wog,	Deer.
Waw-goosh,	Waw-goosh-og,	Fox.
Pezhe-kee,	Pezhe-kee-wog,	Cattle.
Pezhe-keens, (dim.),	Pezhe-keens-og,	Calf.
Aw-ni-moush,	Aw-ni-moush-og,	Dog.
Aw-ni-mouns, (dim.),	Aw-ni-mouns-og,	Puppy.

The plural of inanimate nouns usually terminates in an, en, on, or n.

Sing.	Pl.	Eng.
We-ok-won,	We-ok-won-an,	Hat.
Wig-wom,	Wig-wom-an,	House.
Mo-ke-sin,	Mo-ke-sin-an,	Shoe.
Maw-kok,	Maw-kok-on,	Box.
Maw-kok-ons, (dim.),	Maw-kok-on-son,	Small box.
Tçhi-mawn,	Tchi-mawn-an,	Boat.
Tchi-maw-nes, (dim.),	Tchi maw-nes-on,	Small boat.

Nouns have three cases, nominative, locative and objective. The locative case denotes the relation usually expressed in English by the use of a preposition, or by the genitive, dative and ablative in Latin.

Nom.	Aw-kick,	Kettle.
Loc.	Aw-kick-ong,	In the kettle.
	E-naw-bin aw-kick-ong,	Do look in the kettle.

This relation can be expressed by the word "pin-je," as "Pin-je aw-kick,"—in the kettle; "E-naw-bin pin-je aw-kick,"—do look in the kettle; but this form is seldom used. It is employed only for great emphasis or formality.

The locative termination is "ong," "eng," or "ing."

The objective case is like the nominative when the subject is in the 1st or 2d person, but when the subject is in the 3d person the object takes the termination "won."

Example of locative and objective cases. Chicago is derived from she-gog-ong, the locative case of the Ottawa word she-gog, meaning skunk; nominative, she-gog; locative, she-gog-ong; objective, she-gog or she-gog-won.

Locative case—

She-gog-ong ne-de-zhaw,	I am going to Chicago.
She-gog-ong ne-do-je-baw,	I come from Chicago.
She-gog-ong e-zhawn,	Go to Chicago.

Objective case—

1st p.—She-gog ne-ne-saw,	I kill the skunk.
2d p.—She-gog ke-ne-saw,	You kill the skunk.
3d p.—She-gog-won o-ne-sawn,	He kills the skunk.

Gender is distinguished by the word "quay," either prefixed or added to nouns, to indicate the feminine.

Aw-ne-ne, pl. wog; Man.	Aw-quay, pl. wog; Woman.
Aw-nish-naw-bay; Indian man.	Aw-nesh--naw-bay-quay; I. woman.
Osh-kee-naw-way; Young man.	Osh-kee-ne-ge-quay; Y. woman.
Que-we-zayns, pl. og; Boy.	Quay-zayns, pl. og; Girl.
Aw-yaw-bay-pe-zhe-kee; Bull.	Quay-pe-zhe-kee; Cow.

Proper names always form the feminine by adding "quay."

Ce-naw-day; Irishman.	Ce-naw-day-quay; Irishwoman.

Some genders are irregular.

Aw-ke-wa-zee; Old man. Me-de-mo-gay; Old woman.

Aw-be-non-tchi, an infant, has no distinction of gender.

Os-see-maw, pl. g; Father.	O-gaw-shi-maw, pl. g; Mother.
Me-kaw-ne-see-maw; Brother.	O-me-say-e-maw; Sister.
O-me-shaw-mes-se-maw; Gr.father.	O-kee-mes-se-maw; Grandmother.
O-me-shaw-way-e-maw; Uncle.	O-nou-shay-e-maw; Aunt.
We-taw-wis-see-maw; Male cousin.	We-ne-mo-shay-e-maw; Fem. cous.

Diminutive nouns take the same modifications as the nouns from which they are derived.

Verbs and adjectives are modified to agree with the animate or inanimate nouns to which they belong, as will be illustrated hereafter.

PRONOUNS.

Personal pronouns have no distinction of gender in the third person singular. A peculiarity of this language is the two forms for the first person plural. These two forms for pronouns, and for verbs in all moods and tenses, are like each other except in the first syllable. In one form the first syllable is always "Ke," and in the other "Ne." The form commencing with Ke is used only when speaking to one person, and that commencing with Ne, which might be called the multiple form, is used whenever more than one person is addressed, even though no word may appear in the sentence indicating how many. This is an idiosyncracy which perhaps would never have been developed, certainly would not be perpetuated, in any except an unwritten language. It is of no effect except in a language always colloquial. The multiple form will be given in this grammar as the first person plural, and, whether indicated or not, the other may be understood as being the same with the change of the first syllable from Ne to Ke.

PERSONAL PRONOUNS.

	Sing.		Pl.	
1st p.—Neen or nin,	I,		Ne-naw-wind, (mult.),	We.
			Ke-naw-wind,	We.
2d p.—Keen or kin,	Thou or you,		Ke-naw-waw,	You.
3d p—Ween or win,	He or she,		We-naw-waw,	They.

When these personal pronouns are connected with other words, or when they become subjects or objects of verbs, the first syllable only is used or pronounced. In the third person of verbs the pronoun is entirely omitted.

Sing.		Pl.	
Ne wob,	I see,	Ne wob-me,	We see.
Ke wob,	You see.	Ke wob-em,	You see.
Wo-be,	He or she sees,	Wo-be-wog,	They see.

The whole pronoun is sometimes used when the emphatic or intensive form is desired, as,

Sing.—Neen-ne wob, I myself see.
Keen-ke wob, You yourself see.
Ween wo-be, He himself, or she herself sees.

Pl.—Ne-naw-wind ne-wob-me, We ourselves see.
Ke-naw-waw ke-wob-em, You yourself see.
We-naw-waw wo-be-wog, They themselves see.

POSSESSIVE PRONOUNS.

Ne-daw-yo-em,	Mine;	Ne-daw-yo-em-e-naw,	Ours.
Ke-daw-yo-em,	Thine,	Ke-daw-yo-em-e-waw,	Yours.
O-daw-yo-em,	His or hers,	O-daw-yo-em-e-waw,	Theirs.

Emphatic form—nin ne-daw-yo-em, etc., throughout all the different persons. When these possessive pronouns are used with nouns, nearly all the syllables are omitted, except the first, which is added to the noun in the plural; as—

Sing.		Pl.	
Ne we-ok-won,	My hat,	Ne we-ok-won-e-naw,	Our hat.
Ke we-ok-won,	Your hat,	Ke we-ok-won-e-waw,	Your hat.
O we ok-won,	His hat,	O we-ok-won-e-waw,	Their hat.

The emphatic form, "my own hat," is made by prefixing the personal pronouns, as—

Sing.	Pl.
Neen ne we-ok-won,	Ne-naw-wind ne we-ok-won-e-naw,
Keen ke we-ok-won,	Ke-naw-waw ke we-ok-won-e-waw,
Ween o we-ok-won,	We-naw-waw o we-ok-won-e-waw.

THE IMPERSONAL PRONOUN.

The impersonal pronoun "maw-got," plural "maw-got-on," may be represented by the English impersonal or neuter pronoun it, but it has a wider significance. The inanimate subject of a verb is also represented by maw-got or maw-got-on. Wa-po-tchin-ga maw-got, or wa-po-tchin-ga-sa maw-got, it strikes; plural, wa-po-tchin-ga maw-got-on, or wa-po-tchin-ga-sa maw-got-on, they strike.

Au-no-ke maw-got, It works. Pe-me-say maw-got, It walks.
Ne-bo-we maw-got, It stands. Wo-be maw-got, It sees.
Pe-me-baw-to maw-got, It runs.

Au-nish, interrogative pronoun what; au-naw-tchi, relative pronoun what; e-we, relative pronoun that.

ADJECTIVES.

Adjectives take two forms, to agree with the animate or inanimate nouns to which they belong.

Comparison of adjectives is made by other words: O-ne-zhe-she (inanimate o-ne-zhe-shin), good; Maw-maw-me (or ne-go-ne) o-ne-zhe (or -shin), better; Au-pe-tchi o-ne-zhe-she (or -shin), best. A fourth degree is sometimes used: Maw-mo-me o-ne-zhe-she (or -shin), very best.

The words "Me-no" and "Maw-tchi" or "Mau-tchi," do not change when used with other words, and they are the most common adjectives in the Ottawa and Chippewa languages; they are used as adverbs, as well as adjectives.

"Me-no," is equivalent to good, right, and well; and "Mau-tchi," is equivalent to bad, wicked, evil; as Me-no au-ne.ne, good man; Me-no au-quay, good woman; Me-no au-way-sin, good animal; Me-no au-ky, good land; Me-no waw-bo-yon, good blanket; Me-no e-zhe-wa-be-sy, good behavior, or kind; Me-no au-no-ky, he works well, or doing good business; Me-no pe-maw-de-sy, he is well; Me-no au-yaw, he is getting well, or convalescent from sickness; Me-no au-no-kaw-so-win, good utensil, or handy instrument; Me-no wau-gaw-quat, good ax; Me-no ke-zhi-gut, good day, or pleasant weather; Me-no au-no-kaw-tchi-gon, good goods, or nice goods; Me-no e-zhe-wa-be-sy, he or she is kind or good; Me-no maw-tchaw maw-got, it goes well, etc.

The word "Mau-tchi" is equally useful; as, Mau-tchi au-ne-ne, bad man; Mau-tchi au-quay, bad woman; Mau-tchi e-zhe-wa-be-sy, bad behavior, or wicked person; Mau-tchi mau-ne-to, evil spirit, or the devil; Mau-tchi ke-ge-to, wicked language, or profanity; Mau-tchi wau-gaw-quat, bad ax; Mau-tchi ke-zhwa, vulgar speaker; Mau-tchi no-din, bad wind; Mau-tchi au-naw-quot, bad cloud; Mau-tchi ke-zhe-got, bad day, or rough weather; Mau-tchi wig-wom, bad house, or wicked house; Mau-tchi au-no-ke-win, bad business, etc.

Another adjective equally comprehensive is Kwaw-notch: Kwaw-notch au-ne-ne, well-behaved man; Kwaw-notch au-quay, pretty woman; Kwaw-notch au-no-ke-win, good business; Kwaw-notch au-no-kaw-tchi-gon, nice goods; Kwaw-notchi-won, pretty or nice (inanimate); Kwaw-notchi-we, pretty (animate); Au-pe-tchi kwaw-notchi-we au-quay, very pretty woman.

The following illustrate the changes of form in adjectives for animate and inanimate:

Animate.	Inanimate.	
Me-no-e-zhe-wa-be-sy,	Me-no-e-zhe-wa-bawt,	Kind, mild.
Ke-no-sy,	Ke-nwa,	Long, tall.
Ke-zhe-we-sy,	Ke-zhe-waw,	Hard.
Mush-kaw-we-sy,	Mush-kaw-waw,	Strong.
Ke-zhe-kaw, or ke-zhe-be-so,	Ke-zhe-be-ta,	Swift, fleet.
Ko-se-gwan-ny,	Ko-se-gwan,	Heavy.
Maw-tchi-e-zhe-wa-be-sy,	Maw-tchi-e-zhe-wa-bot,	Bad.
Ma-tchaw-yaw-au-wish,	Ma-tchaw-yaw-e-wish,	Wicked.

We-saw-ge-sy,	We-saw-gun,	Bitter.
Wish-ko-be-sy,	Wish-ko-bun,	Sweet.
Sou-ge-sy,	Sou-gun,	Tough.
Se-we-sy,	Se-won,	Sour.
Maw-kaw-te-we-sy,	Maw-kaw-te-waw,	Black.
Ozaw-we-sy,	Ozaw-waw,	Yellow.
Ozhaw-wash-ko-sy,	Ozhaw-wash-kwaw,	Green.
Mis-ko-sy,	Mis-kwa,	Red.
We-bin-go-sy,	We-bin-gwaw,	Blue.
O-zaw won-so,	O-zaw won-day,	Yellow color.
Maw-kaw-te won-so,	Maw-kaw-te won-day,	Black color.

Maw-kaw-te au-ne-ne, black man. Maw-kaw-te mo-kok, black box.
Mis-ko au-ne-ne, red man. Mis-ko wau-bo-yon, red blanket.

It will be observed that the last one or two syllables of the adjective are dropped when in connection with a noun.

VERBS.

Ottawa and Chippewa verbs are changed in their conjugations, to indicate—

1st. Whether their subjects are animate, or inanimate;
2d. Whether their objects are animate, or inanimate;
3d. Whether they are transitive, or intransitive;
4th. Whether they are active, or passive, or reflective;
5th. Whether the expression is common, or emphatic.

They also express by their forms all of the distinctions of mood and tense, person and number, found in the English, and form their participles, and are changed into verbal or participial nouns; and these modifications are for the most part regular in form.

I. Verbs with inanimate subjects correspond to English impersonal or neuter verbs, but are much more extensively used. They are usually formed by adding the impersonal pronoun, maw-got—it; as,

Animate Subject.	Inanimate Subject.
Sing. Au-nou-kee, he works.	Au-nou-ke-maw-got, it works.
Ke-au-nou-ke, he worked.	Ke-au-nou-ke-maw-got, it worked.

Plu. Au-nou-ke-wog, they work. Au-nou-ke-maw-go-toun, things wrk
Ke-au-nou-ke-wog, " wrk'd. Ke-au-nou-ke-maw-go-toun, " wrkd.

Standing trees, as well as all liviug creatures and personified things, are regarded as animate.

II, III. The distinctions for animate and inanimate objects, and for transitive and intransitive, are illustrated by the following:

Singular—I kill, Thou killest, etc.

Pers.	Intransitive.	Transitive. Animate Object.	Inanimate Object.
1	Ne-ne-taw-gay	Ne-ne-saw	Ne-ne-ton
2	Ke-ne-taw-gay	Ke-ne-saw	Ke-ne-toun
3	Ne-taw-gay	O-ne-sawn, or son	O-ne-toun
	Plural—We kill, You kill, etc.		
1	Ne-ne-taw-gay-me	Ne-ne-saw-naw	Ne-ne-tou-naw
2	Ke-ne-taw-gaym	Ke-ne-saw-waw	Ke-ne-tou-naw-waw
3	Ne-taw-gay-wog	O-ne-saw-wawn or won	O-ne-tou-naw-waw
	Singular—I see, Thou seest, etc.		
1	Ne-waub	Ne-waub-maw	Ne-waub-don, or dawn
2	Ke-waub	Ke-waub-maw	Ke-waub-don "
3	Wau-be	O-waub-mon, or mawn	O-waub-don "
	Plural—We see, You see, etc.		
1	Ne-waub-me	Ne-waub-maw-naw	Ne-waub-daw-naw
2	Ke-wau-bem	Ke-waub-maw-waw	Ke-waub-daw-naw-wan
3	Wau-be-wog	O-waub-naw-won	O-waub-daw-naw-wan

IV. What is denominated the reflective form of the verb, is where the subject and the object are the same person or thing; as, in English, He hates himself. The passive and reflective forms are illustrated in the verb, To See, thus:

Passive.	Reflective.
Ne-wob-me-go, I am seen.	Ne-wau-baw-dis, I see myself.
Ke-wob-me-go, thou art seen.	Ke-wau-baw-dis, thou seest thyself.
Wob-maw, he is seen.	Wau-baw-de-so, he sees himself.
Ne-wob-me-go-me, we are seen.	Ne-wau-baw-de-so-me, we s. ourslvs.
Ke-wob-me-gom, you are seen.	Ke-wau-baw-de-som, you s. yourslvs
Wob-maw-wag, they are seen.	Wau-baw-de-so-wag, they s. thmslvs

V. The emphatic form repeats the first part of the pronoun; as, Ne-waub, I see; Nin-ne-waub, I do see (literally, I myself see).

Intransitive.

	Common Form—I eat, etc.	Emphatic Form—I do eat, etc.
1	Ne-we-sin	Nin-ne-we-sin
2	Ke-we-sin	Kin-ke-we-sin
3	We-se-ne	Win-we-we-sin

Transitive—Animate Object.

1	Ne-daw-mwaw	Nin-ne-daw-mwaw
2	Ke-daw-mwaw	Kin-ke-daw-mwaw
3	O-daw-mwaw	Win-o-daw-mwaw

Transitive—Inanimate Object.

1	Ne-me-djin	Nin-ne-me-djin
2	Ke-me-djin	Kin-ke-me-djin
3	O-me-djin	Win-o-me-djin

The object is frequently placed before the verb—always when in answer to a questiou. Thus, the answer to the question, What is he eating? would be, Ke-goon-yan o-daw-mwawn—Fish he is eating.

Nouns are formed from verbs by adding "win"; as, waub, to see, wau-be-win, sight; paw-pe, to laugh, paw-pe-win, laughter; au-no-ke, to work, au-no-ke-win, labor.

NOTE.—A verb susceptible of both the transitive and intransitive office, and of both animate and inanimate subjects, as, for instance, the verb To Blow, may have no less than fifteen forms for the indicative present third person singular. The intransitive may be both animate and inanimate as to subject, and the former both common and emphatic; the transitive would have the same, multiplied by animate and inanimate objects; and the passive and reflective would each have inanimate, and common and emphatic animate—fifteen. Double these for the plural, and we have thirty forms; and that multiplied by the sixteen tenses of the indicative, potential and subjunctive moods gives 480 forms of third person. The first and second persons have the same, minus the inanimate subject, or 20 each for each tense, making 640 more, or 1120 all together in those three moods. The imperative singular and plural, and the infinitive present and past, and the participles, add 25. Then there is the additional form for the first person plural, treated under "Pronouns," running through all the sixteen tenses, common and emphatic, animate and inanimate and intransitive, 96 more —making the astonishing number of 1241 forms of a single verb!—[EDITOR.

Conjugation of the Verb To Be.

INDICATIVE MOOD.

Pers.	Singular.	Plural.
	Present Tense—I am, etc.	
1	Ne-daw-yaw	Ne-daw-yaw-me
2	Ke-daw-yaw	Ke-daw-yaw-me
3	Aw-yaw	Aw-yaw-waug or wog
	Imperfect Tense—I was, etc.	
1	Ne-ge-au-yaw	Ne-ge-au-yaw-me
2	Ke-ge-au-yaw	Ke-ge-au-yawm
3	Ke-au-yaw	Ke-au-yaw-wog
	Perfect Tense—I have been, etc.	
1	Au-zhe-gwaw ne-ge-au-yaw	Au-zhe-gwaw ne-ge-au-yaw-me
2	Au-zhe-gwaw ke-ge-au-yaw	Au-zhe-gwaw ke-ge-au-yawm
3	Au-zhe-gwaw ke-au-yaw	Au-zhe-gwaw ke-au-yaw-wog
	Pluperfect Tense—I had been, etc.	
1	Ne-ge-au-yaw-naw-baw	Ne-ge-au-me-naw-baw
2	Ke-ge-au-yaw-naw-baw	Ke-ge-au-me-naw-baw
3	Ke-au-yaw-baw	Ke-au-yaw-baw-neg
	Future Tense—I shall or will be, etc.	
1	Ne-gaw-au-yaw	Ne-gaw-au-yaw-me
2	Ke-gaw-au-yaw	Ke-gaw-au-yawm
3	Taw-au-yaw	Taw-au-yaw-wag

POTENTIAL MOOD.

Pers.	Singular.	Plural.
	Present Tense—I may or can be, etc.	
1	Ko-maw ne-taw-au-yaw	Ko-maw ne-taw-au-yaw-me
2	Ko-maw ke-taw-au-yaw	Ko-maw ke-taw-au-yawm
3	Ko-maw tau-yaw	Ko-maw taw-au-yo-wog
	Imperfect Tense—I might be, etc.	
1	Ko-maw ne-ge-au-yaw	Ko-maw ne-ge-au-yaw-me
2	Ko-maw ke-ge-au-yaw	Ko-maw ke-ge-au-yom
3	Ko-maw ke-au-yaw	Ko-maw ke-au-yaw-wog
	Perfect Tense—I may have been, etc.	
1	Au-zhe-gwau ne-tau-ge-au-yaw	Au-zhe-gwau ne-tau-ge-au-yaw-me
2	Au-zhe-gwau ke-tau-ge-au-yaw	Au-zhe-gwau ke-tau-ge-au-yawm
3	Au-zhe-gwau tau-ge-au-yaw	Au-zhe-gwau tau-ge-au-yaw-og

Pluperfect Tense—I might have been, etc.

1 Ko-maw au-yaw-yom-baw   Ko maw au-yaw-wong-ge-baw
2 Ko-maw ke-au-yaw-yom-baw   Ko-maw au-yaw-ye-go-baw
3 Ko-maw au-yaw-go-baw-nay   Ko-maw au-yaw-wo-go-baw-nay

SUBJUNCTIVE MOOD.

Present Tense—If I be, etc.

1 Tchish-pin au-yaw-yaw   Tchish-pin au-yaw-wong
2 Tchish-pin au-yaw-yon   Tchish-pin au-yaw-yeg
3 Tchish-pin au-yawd   Tchish-pin au-yaw-wod

Imperfect Tense—If I were, etc.

1 Tchish-pin ke-au-yaw-yaw   Tchish-pin ke-au-yaw-wong
2 Tchish-pin ke-au-yaw-yon   Tchish-pin ke-au-yaw-yeg
3 Tchish-pin ke-au-yawd   Tchish-pin ke-au-yaw-wod

Perfect Tense—If I have been, etc.

1 Tchish-pin au-zhe-gaw ke-au-yaw-yaw
2 Tchish-pin au-zhe-gaw ke-au-yaw-yon
3 Tchish-pin au-zhe-gwa ke-au-yawd
Tchish-pin au-zhe-gwa ke-aw-yaw-wog
Tchish-pin au-zhe-gwa ke-au-yaw-yeg
Tchish-pin au-zhe-gwa ke-au-yaw-wod

[The syllable "gwa" is often omitted, merely saying, "au-zhe."]

Pluperfect Tense—If I had been, etc.

1 Au-zhe ke-au-yaw-yaw-baw   Au-zhe ke-au-yaw-wong-o-baw
2 Au-zhe ke-au-yaw-yawm-baw   Au-zhe ke-au-yaw-ye-go-baw
3 Au-zhe ke-au-yaw-paw   Au-zhe ke-au-yaw-wau-paw

Future Tense—If I shall or will be, etc.

1 Tchish-pin we-au-yaw-yaw   Tchish-pin we-au-yaw-wong
2 Tchish-pin we-au-yaw-yon   Tchish-pin we-au-yaw-yeg
3 Tchish-pin we-au-yawd   Tchish-pin we-au-yaw-wod

IMPERATIVE MOOD—Be thou, Do you be.

2 Au-yawm   Au-yawg

INFINITIVE MOOD—To be, To have been.

Present—Tchi-au-yong   Perfect—Au-zhe tchi-ke-au-yong

PARTICIPLES—Being, Been, Having been.

Au-zhaw-yong   Tchi-ge-au-yong   Au-zhe-gwaw tchi-ge-au-yong

Synopsis of the Verb To See.

I see, Ne-wob. I saw, Ne-ge-wob.
I have seen, Au-zhe-gwaw ne-ge-wob. I had s'n, Ne-ge-wob-naw-baw
I shall see, Ne-gaw-wob. I shall have seen, Au-zhe-ge-wob.
I may see, Ko-maw ne-taw-wob. I might see, Ko-maw ne-ge-wob.
I may have seen, Au-zhe-gwaw ne-taw-ge-wob.
I might have seen, Ko-maw wob-yawm-baw.
If I see, Tchish-pin wob-yon. If I saw, Tchish-pin ke-wob-yon-baw.
If I have seen, Tchish-pin au-zhe-gwa wob-yon.
If I had seen, Tchish-pin ke-wob-yon-baw.
If I shall see, Tchish-pin we-wob-yon.
If I shall have seen, Tchish-pin we-wob-yon-baw.
See thou, Wob-ben. To see, Tchi-wob-bing.
To have seen, Tchi-ge-wob-bing. Seeing, Au-wob-bing.
Having seen, Au-zhe-gwaw au-ge-wob-bing.
Having been seen, Au-ge-wob-bing-e-baw.
I am seen, Ne-wob-me-go. I was seen, Ne-ge-wob-me-go.
I have been seen, Au-zhe ne-ge-wob-me-go.
I had been seen, Ne-ge-wob-me-go-naw-baw.
I shall be seen, Ne-gaw-wob-me-go.
I shall have been seen, She-gwa-we-wob-me-go-yon.
I may be seen, Ko-maw wob-me-go-yon.
I might be seen, Ko-maw ke-wob-me-go-yon.
I may have been seen, Ko-maw au-zhe ke-wob-me-go-yon.
I might have been seen, Ko-maw au-zhe ke-wob-me-go-yon-baw.
If I be seen, Tchish-pin wob-em-go-yon.
If I have been seen, Tchish-pin au-zhe ke-wob-me-go-yon.
If I had been seen, Tchish-pin ke-wob-me-go-yon-baw.
If I shall be seen. Tchish-pin we-wob-me-go-yon.
If I shall have been seen, Tchish-pin she-gwa-we-wob-me-go-yon.
I see myself, Ne-wau-baw-dis. I saw myself, Ne-ge-wau-baw-dis.
I shall see myself, Ne-gaw-wau-baw-dis.
I may see myself, Ko-maw ne-daw-wau-baw-dis.
See thyself, Wau-baw-de-son. To see thyself, Tchi-wob-on-di-song.

MINOR PARTS OF SPEECH.

Adverbs: When, au-pe, au-ne-nish; where, au-ne-pe, au-ne-zhaw; there, e-wo-te, au-zhe-we. [The significance of the double forms is not clear; and comparison, as with Adjectives, seems to be by different words.—Ed.]

Prepositions are few, and are oftener embraced in the form of the verb, as in the Latin. The most important are, pin-je, in; tchish-pin, or kish-pin, if. Po-taw-wen pin-je ke-zhap ke-ze-gun, make some fire in the stove; Tchish-pin maw-tchawt, if he go away. Or the same may be expressed, Po-taw-wen ke-zhap ke-ze-gun-ing ("ing" forming locative case, with the preposition implied); and, Maw-yaw-tchaw-gwen (the latter form of verb expressing subjunctive mood). The employment of the preposition makes the expression more emphatic.

The most important Conjunctions are, haw-yea, gaw-ya, ka-ie, and; and ke-maw, or. [Three forms of "and" doubtless due to imperfect orthography.]

Interjections embrace, yaw! exclamation of danger; au-to-yo! surprise; a-te-way! disappointment; taw-wot-to! disgust; ke-yo-o! disgust (used only by females).

There is no Article; but the words, mondaw, that, and maw-baw, this, are often used before nouns as specifying terms, and are always emphatic. E-we is common for that, directed to things at a distance.

A peculiarity, of uncertain significance, is the termination, sh, or esh, employed in connection with the possessive case. It does not change the interpretation, and is perhaps an expression of familiarity, or intimate relationship. Illustration:

Ne-gwiss, my son;	Ne-gwiss-esh, my son.
Ne-daw-niss, my daughter;	Ne-daw-niss-esh, my daughter.
Ne-dib, my head;	Ne-dib-awsh, my head.
Ne-wau-bo-yon, my blanket;	Ne-wau bo-yon-esh, my blanket.
Ne-gwiss-og, my sons;	Ne-gwiss-es-shog, my sons.
Ne-daw-niss-og, my daughters;	Ne-daw-niss-es-shog, my da'ght'rs.

VOCABULARIES.

One,	Pa-zhig.	Ten,	Me-toss-we.
Two,	Nezh.	Twenty,	Nezh-to-naw.
Three,	Ness-we.	Thirty,	Ne-se-me-to-naw.
Four,	Ne-win.	Forty,	Ne-me-to-naw.
Five,	Naw-non.	Fifty,	Naw-ne-me-to-naw.
Six,	Ne-go-twos-we.	Sixty,	Ne-go-twa-se-me-to-naw.
Seven,	Nezh-was-we.	Seventy,	Nezh-wo-se-me-to-naw.
Eight,	Nish-shwas-we.	Eighty,	Nish-wo-se-me-to-naw.
Nine,	Shong-swe.	Ninety,	Shong-gaw-se-me-to-naw.

One hundred, Go-twok.

Father,	Os-se-maw, pl. g.	Mother,	O-gaw-shi-maw, pl.g.
Brother,	We-kaw-ne-se-maw.	Sister,	O-me-say-e-maw.
Gr'father,	O-me-shaw-mes-e-maw.	Gr'mother,	O-ko-mes-se-maw.
Cousin,m.	We-taw-wis-e-maw.	Cousin,fm.,	We-ne-mo-shay-emaw
Uncle,	O-me-shaw-may-e-maw	Aunt,	O-nou-shay-e-maw.
Boy,	Que-we-zayns, pl. og.	Girl,	Quay-zayns, pl. og.
Man,	Au-ne-ne, pl. wog.	Woman,	Au-quay, pl. wog.
Old man,	Au-ke-wa-ze, pl. yog.	Old woman,	Me-de-mo-yay, yog.

Ae, yes.	Kau, no.	Nau-go, now.
Ka-ge-te, truly so.	Kau-win, no (emphatic).	Au-zhon-daw, here.
Pe-nau! hark!	Ka-go, don't.	E-wo-te, there.
Pa-kau, stop.	Kaw-ga-go, none.	Ne-gon, before.

Aush-kwe-yong, behind.	Ne-se-wo-yaw-ing, between.
Pe-tchi-naw-go, yesterday.	Wau-bung, to-morrow.
Pe-tchi-nog, just now.	Wau-e-baw, soon.
Au-no-maw-yaw, lately.	Way-wib, quickly.
Au-gaw-won, hardly.	Naw-a-gotch, slowly.
Au-pe-tchi, very.	O-je-daw, purposely.
Kay-gaw, almost.	Saw-kou, for example.
Mou-zhawg, always.	Me-naw-gay-kaw! to be sure!
Ne-sawb, alike.	Kaw-maw-me-daw, can't.
Pin-dig, inside.	Pin-di-gayn, come in.

WE-YAW,	THE BODY.	PE-NAY-SHEN, †	BIRD.
O-dib,	Head.	Wing-ge-zee,	Eagle.
O-te-gwan,	Face.	Pe-nay-se,	Hawk.
O-don,	Mouth.	Mong,	Loon.
Osh-ke-zheg,	Eye.	Me-zhe-say,	Turkey.
O-no-wau-e,*	Cheek.	She-sheb,	Duck.
Otch-awsh,	Nose.	Kaw-yawshk,	Gull.
O-daw-me-kon,	Jaw.	Tchin-dees,	Bluejay.
O-da-naw-naw,	Tongue.	May-may,	Woodcock.
We-bid,	Tooth.	Pe-nay,	Partridge.
We-ne-zes,	Hair.	Au-dje-djawk,	Crane.
O-kaw-tig,	Forehead.	O-me-me,	Pigeon.
O-maw-maw,	Eyebrow.	Au-pe-tchi,	Robin.
Kaw-gaw-ge,*	Palate.	Awn-dayg,	Crow.
O-kaw-gun,	Neck.	Au-nawk,	Thrasher.
O-do-daw-gun,	Throat.	Paw-paw-say,	Woodpecker.
O-pe-kwawn,	Back.	Ke-wo-nee,	Prairie hen.
O-pe-gay-gun,	Rib.	MAW-KWA,	BEAR.
O-me-gawt,	Stomach,	Mooz,	Moose.
O-naw-gish,	Bowel.	Me-shay-wog,	Elk.
Osh-kawt,	Belly.	Maw-in-gawn,	Wolf.
O-kwan,	Liver.	Au-mick,	Beaver.
O-kun,	Bone.	Maw-boos,	Rabbit.
O-nenj,	Hand.	Pe-zhen,	Lynx.
O-neek,	Arm.	Au-ni-moosh,	Dog.
O-dos-kwon,	Elbow.	Au-ni-mouns,	Puppy.
O-kawd,	Leg.	Au-zhawshk,	Muskrat.
O-ge-dig,*	Knee.	Wau-goosh,	Fox.
O bwom,	Thigh.	Shaw-gway-she.	Mink.
O-zeet,	Foot.	A-se-bou,	Raccoon.
O-don-dim,	Heel.	Me-she-be-zhe,‡	Panther.
O-ge-tchi-zeet,	Big toe.	She-gos-se,	Weasel.
O-ge-tchi-nenj,	Thumb.	Au-saw-naw-go,	Squirrel.

* Pl. og; others an.

† Pl. yog; ‡ eg; others wog, og, g.

KE-GON,* Fish.
Ke-gons† (dim.), minnow.
Naw-me-gons, trout,
Maw-zhaw-me-gons, brook trout,
Maw-may, sturgeon.
O-gaw, pickerel.
She-gwaw-meg, dog fish.
Au-saw-way, perch.
O-kay-yaw-wis, herring.
Au-she-gun, black bass.
Au-de-kaw-meg, whitefish.
Ke-no-zhay, pike.
Paw-zhe-toun,* sheep head.
Maw-maw-bin, sucker.

MAW-NE-TONS, insect.
O-jee, house fly.
Me-ze-zawk, horse fly.
Au-mon, bumblebee.
Au-moans (dim.), bee, hornet.
May-may-gwan,* butterfly.
Au-kou-jesh, louse.
Paw-big, flea.
O-ze-gog, woodtick.
A-naw-go, ant.
A-a-big, spider.
Saw-ge-may, mosquito.
Mo-say, cut worm.
O-quay, maggot.

* Pl. yog; † sog; others wog, og, g.

Paw-gawn, nut; (dim. paw-gaw-nays, hazelnut or other small nut)
Au-zhaw-way-mish, pl. eg; beech tree.
Au-zhaw-way-min, pl. on; beech nut.
Me-te-gwaw-bawk, pl. og; hickory tree.
Me-gwaw-baw-ko paw-gon, pl. on; hickory nut.
Paw-gaw-naw-ko paw-gon, pl. on; walnut.
Me-she-me-naw-gaw-wosh, pl. eg; apple tree.
Me-she-min, pl. og; apple.
Shaw-bo-me-naw-gaw-wosh, pl. eg; gooseberry bush.
Shaw-bo-min, pl. og; gooseberry.
Paw-gay-saw-ne-mish, pl. eg; plum tree.
Paw-gay-son, pl. og; plum.
Aw-nib, pl. eg; elm.
Shin-gwawk, pl. wog; pine.
Au-bo-yawk, pl. wog; ash.
Me-daw-min, pl. og; corn.
Aw-doup, pl. eg; willow.
Ke-zhek, pl. og; cedar.
We-saw-gawk, pl. og; black ash.
O-zaw-o-min, pl. og; yellow corn.
Mis-kou-min, pl. og; red raspberry.
Wau-be-mis-kou-min, pl. og; white raspberry.
Wau-kaw-tay-mis-kou-min, pl. og; black raspberry.

AU-KEE; the world, the earth, land, country, soil.
Pay-maw-te-se-jeg au-king, the people of the world.
Taw-naw-ke-win, country or native land.
Ke-taw-kee-me-naw, our country.
Maw-kaw-tè au-kee, black earth or soil.
Me-daw-keem, my land.
Au-ke-won, soiled; also applied to rich land.
Ne-besh, water; ne-be-kaw, wet land.
Wau-bawsh-ko-kee, marsh land.
Au-ke-kaw-daw-go-kee, tamarack swamp.
Ke-zhe-ke-kee, cedar swamp.
Au-tay yaw-ko-kee, swamp, swampy land.
Shen-gwaw-ko-kee, pine land.
Ne-gaw-we-kee, sand; ne-gaw-we-kaw, sandy.
Kong-ke-tchi-gaw-me, the ocean.
Ke-tchi-au-gaw-ming, across the ocean.
Se-be (pl. won), river; se-be-wens (dim), (pl. an,) brook.
Ke-te-gawn (pl. on), farm; ke-te-gaw-nes (dim.), garden.
Ke-te-gay we-ne-ne, (pl. wog), farmer.
Ke-zes, sun; te-bik-ke-zes, moon; au-nong (pl. wog), star.
Ke-zhe-gut, day; te-be-kut, night.
Ne-bin, summer; pe-boon, winter.
Ne-be-nong, last summer; me-no-pe-boon, pleasant winter.
Tau-gwan-gee, fall; me-nou-kaw-me, spring.
Au-won-se-me-nou-kaw-ming, year ago last spring.
Maw-tchi taw-gwan-ge, bad or unpleasant fall.
No-din, wind; no-wau-yaw, the air.
No-de-naw-ne-mot, windy.
To-ke-sin, calm; ne-tche-wod, stormy.
Au-pe-tchi ne-tche-wod, very stormy.
Wig-wom, house; wig-wom-an, houses.
Au-sin wig-wom, stone house.
Au-naw-me-a-we-gaw-mig, a church.
Te-baw-ko-we-ga we-gaw-mig, a court house.

Me-no-say, handy. — Me-no-sayg, that which is handy.

Au-no-ke, work. — A-no-ket, he that is working.

Wo-be, he sees. — Wau-yaw-bet, he that sees.

Pe-mo-say, he walks. — Pe-mo-sayt, he that is walking.

Pe-me-bot-to, he runs. — Pe-me-bot-tot, he that runs.

Get him, nawzh. — Get it, naw-din.

Help him, naw-daw-maw. — Help it, naw-daw-maw-don.

Call him, naw-doum. — Ask for it, naw-dou-don.

Go to him, naw-zhe-kow. — Go to it, naw-zhe-kon.

Meet him, naw-kwesh-kow. — Meet it, naw-kwesh-kon.

Ne-dje-mon, my boat. — Ne-dje-may, I paddle.

Ne-dje-bawm, my soul. — Ne-do-ge-mom, my master.

Ne-gwes, my son. — Ne-daw-nes, my daughter.

Ne-taw-wes, my cousin. — Ne-kaw-nes, my brother.

Ne-daw-kim, my land. — Ne-ne-tchaw-nes, my child.

He sleeps, ne-baw. — He is dead, ne-bou.

He is sleepy, au-kon-gwa-she. — He died, ke-ne-bou.

He is white, wau-besh-ke-zee. — He is afraid, sa-ge-ze.

He is lonely, aush-ken-dom. — He is lazy, ke-te-mesh-ke.

He is killed, nes-saw. — He is well, me-no-pe-maw-de-ze.

Ne-tawn, first. — Ne-tawm ke-taw-gwe-shin, he came first.

Ne-gon, before. — Ne-gon-ne, he goes before.

Au-ko-zee, sick. — Au-ko-ze-we-gaw-mig, hospital.

Au-gaw-saw, small. — O-gaw-sawg o-naw-gun pe-ton, bring small [plate.

Au-gaw-won, scarcely. — Au-gaw-won ne-wob, I scarcely see.

Once, ne-go-ting. — Only once, ne-go-ting a-taw.

Not there, ne-go-tchi. — Look elsewhere, ne-go-tchi e-naw-bin.

Change, mesh-kwot. — He is elsewhere, ne-go-tchi e-zhaw.

Full, mosh-ken. — It is elsewhere, ne-go-tchi au-tay.

Fill it, mosh-ke-naw-don. — Change it, mes-kwo-to-non.

Saw-kon, go out. — Pe-saw-kon, come out.

Maw-tchawn, go away. — Pe-maw-tchawn, come away.

Pe-to, to bring. — Pe-ton, fetch it.

Ash-kom, more and more.
Ash-kom so-ge-po, more and more snow.
Ash-kom ke-me-wau, " " rain.
Ash-kom ke-zhaw-tay, hotter and hotter.
Ash-kom ke-se-naw, colder and colder.
E-ke-to, saying.
E-ke-to, he says.

Nos, my father.
Kos, your father.
O-sawn, his father.
Ne-gaw-she, my mother.
Ke-gaw-she, your mother.
E-ke-ton, say it.
Ke-e-ke-to, he said.

Kay-go mon-daw e-ke-to-kay, do not say that.
E-wau, he says [the same as e-ke-to, but used only in third person and cannot be conjugated].
E-naw-bin, look; e-naw-bin au-zhon-daw, look here.
A-zhawd, going; au-ne-pe a-zhawd? where did he go?
E-wo-te, there; me-saw e-wo-te au-daw-yon, there is your home.
Au-zhe-me, there; au-zhe-me au-ton, set it there.
Au-ne-me-kee, thunder; au-ne-me-ke-kaw, it thundered.
Awsh-kon-tay, fire; awsh-kon-tay o-zhe-ton, make some fire.
On-je-gaw, leaked; on-je-gaw tchi-mon, the boat leaked.
Kaw-ke-naw, all; kaw-ke-naw ke-ge-way-wog, all gone home.
Ke-wen, go home. [This verb always implies home, but the emphatic expression is ke-wen en-daw-yawn.]
Son-gon (inanimate), son-ge-ze (animate), tough.
Se-gwan, spring; se-gwa-nong, last spring (Chippewa dialect).
Me-gwetch, thanks; me-gwe-tchi-me-au, he is thanked.
Taw-kwo, short; on-sawm taw-kwo, too short.
Ke-me-no-pe-maw-tis naw? Are you well?
Ae, ne-me-no-pe-maw-tis. Yes, I am well.
Ke-taw-kos naw? Are you sick?
Kau-win ne-taw-ko-si-sy. No, I am not sick.
Au-ne-pish kos e-zhat? Where did your father go?
O-day-naw-wing ezhaw. He is gone to town.
Ke-ge-we-sin naw? Have you eaten?
Ae, ne-ge-aush-kwaw-we-sin. Yes, I have done eating.
Ke-baw-kaw-tay naw? Are you hungry?
Kaw-win, ne-baw-kaw-tay-sy. No, I am not hungry.

Pe-mo-say-win, walking (noun); ne-pe-mo-say, I walk.
Aum-bay paw-baw-mo-say-taw, let us go walking.
Ne-ge-paw-baw-mo-say, I have been walking.
Ne-ge-paw-baw-mish-kaw, I have been boat riding.
Aum-bay paw-baw-mish-kaw-daw, let us go boat riding.
Maw-tchawn, go on, or go away.
Maw-tchawn we-wib, go on quickly.
Ke-maw-tchaw-wog, the have gone.
Aum-bay maw-tchaw-taw, let us go.
Wau-saw e-zhaw, he is gone far away.
We-kau-de-win, a feast; we-koum, I invite him (to a feast).
We-kau-maw-wog, they are invited (to a feast).
Maw-zhe-aw, overpowered; maw-zhe-twaw, victorious.
Mou-dje-ge-ze-win, or, me-naw-wo-ze-win, rejoicing.
Mou-dje-ge-ze, or, me-naw-wo-ze, he rejoices.
Au-no-maw-yaw ke-daw-gwe-shin, he came lately.
Au-pe-tchi ke-zhaw-tay, it is very hot.
Ke-tchi no-din, it is blowing hard.
Paw-ze-gwin we-wib, get up quickly.
Me-no e-naw-kaw-me-got, good news.
Me-no e-naw-kaw-me-got naw? Is it good news?
She-kaw-gong ne-de-zhaw-me, we are going to Chicago.
She-kaw-gong on-je-baw, he came from Chicago
Saw-naw-got, difficult to overcome.
Saw-naw-ge-ze, he is in difficulty.
Saw-naw-ge-ze-wog, they are in difficulty.
Sa-ge-ze, he is frightened; sa-ge-ze-win, fright.
Ke-gus-kaw-naw-baw-gwe naw? Are you thirsty?
Au-pe-tchi ne-gus-kaw-naw-gwe. I am very thirsty.
Me-naw au-we, give him drink.
Ne-bish me-naw, give him water to drink.
O-daw-kim o-ge-au-taw-wen, he sold his land.
O-da paw-gaw-awn, the heart beats.
O-da me-tchaw-ne, he has a big heart.

Ke-ne-se-to-tom naw? Do you understand?
Ke-ne-se-to-tow naw? Do you understand me?
Kau-win, ke-ne-se to-tos-no. No, I do not understand you.
Ke-no-dom naw? Do you hear? Ae, ne-no-dom. Yes, I hear.
Ke-pe-sen-dom naw? Do you listen?
Ke-maw-ne-say naw? Are you chopping?
Maw-tchi e-naw-kaw-me-got naw? Is it bad news?
We-go-nash wau-au-yaw mon? What do you want?
Au-nish au-pe-daw-taw-gwe-she non? When did you come
Au-ne-pesh a-zhaw yon? Where are you going?
Au-ne-pesh wen-dje-baw yon? Where are you from
Au-ne-dosh wau-e-ke-to yon? What shall you say?
Au-nish mon-daw e-naw-gen deg? What is the price?
Maw-ne-say, he chops; ma-ne-sayt, he that chops.
Ne-bwa-kaw, wise; ne-bwa-kawt, he that is wise.
Na-bwa-kaw-tchig, they that are wise.
Wa-zhe-tou-tchig awsh-kou-te, they that make fire.

O-zhe-tou aush-ko-tay pin-je ke-zhaw-be-ke-se-gun,
Make fire in the stove.

Wen-daw-mow way-naw-paw-nod au-zhon-daw,
Tell him the cheap place is here.

Wen-daw-mow e-naw-kaw-me-gok, tell him the news.

Taw-bes-kaw-be.	Taw-be-e-shaw au-zhon-daw.
He will come back.	He will come here.
On-je-baw.	Wow-kwing on-je-baw.
Coming from.	He comes from heaven.

Nau-go, now; nau-go a-ge-zhe-gok, to-day.
Te-besh-kou, same, even; ta-te-besh-kon, even with the other.
To-dawn mon-daw e-ne-taw, do that as I tell you.
Pe-sen-dow, listen to him; pe-sen-do-we-shin, listen to me.

Me-saw-wen-dje-gay.	Me-saw-me-dje-gay-win.
He covets.	Coveting.

E-zhaw-yon gaw-ya ne-ne-gaw e-zhaw.
If you will go and also I will go.

O-je-daw ne-ge-to-tem tchi-baw-ping.
Purposely I did it to make laughter.

Kaw-win ke-taw-gawsh-ke-to-se tchi-gaw-ke-so-taw-wod mau-ni-to, you cannot hide from God.

Maw-no-a-na-dong taw-e-zhe-tchi-gay, let him do what he thinks.

A-naw-bid. E-naw-bin a-naw-bid.
In the way he looks. Do look in the way he looks.

Au-nish a-zhe-wa-bawk mon-daw?
What is the matter with that?

Au-nish a-zhe-we-be-sit au-we?
What is the matter with him?

Au-nish a-naw-tchi-moo-tawk?
What did he tell you?

E-zhaw. Au-ne-pish kaw-e-zhawd?
He went. Where did he go?

E-zhaw-wog. Harbor Springs ke-e-zhaw-wog.
They went. They went to Harbor Springs.

Ne-daw-yaw-naw e-naw-ko-ne-ga-win.
We have a rule, or, a law.

O-we-o-kwon o-ge-au-taw-son.
His hat he pawned.

Ne-be-me-baw-to-naw-baw au-pe pen-ge-she-naw.
I was running when I fell.

NOTE.—Except some condensation and arrangement in the grammar, this work is printed almost verbatim as written by the author.—EDITOR.